Untying YESTERDAY'S KNOTS

Walking with God in Rundown Sneakers

Rita Cato Cochrane

Untying Yesterday's Knots
ISBN: 978-0-89098-941-8

©2024 by 21st Century Christian
4108 Hillsboro Pike, Nashville, TN 37215

Scripture quotations marked (NIV) are taken from the Holy Bible, New International Version®, NIV®. Copyright © 1973, 1978, 1984, 2011 by Biblica, Inc.™ Used by permission of Zondervan. All rights reserved worldwide. www.zondervan.com The "NIV" and "New International Version" are trademarks registered in the United States Patent and Trademark Office by Biblica, Inc.™

Scripture quotations marked (ESV) are from The ESV® Bible (The Holy Bible, English Standard Version®), copyright © 2001 by Crossway, a publishing ministry of Good News Publishers. Used by permission. All rights reserved.

Scripture taken from the New King James Version®. Copyright © 1982 by Thomas Nelson. Used by permission. All rights reserved.

Cover design by 21st Century Christian Editorial Team

Author Photo by MBCochrane Photography

TABLE OF CONTENTS

4

Preface

Dear friend, I am delighted you have chosen to join me in this study. The chapters in this book are taken from the lives of those who live on the inspired pages of our Bibles. If you think, however, we will study perfect people making perfect choices as they walk through their perfect lives, you may be quite disappointed. Instead, we will inspect the lives of completely imperfect people who made some complete messes of their lives, yet our perfect God used them to do His perfect work anyway.

It might seem the highs and lows of the men and women who live in Scripture have little in common with our modern, fast-food, hurry-up world. However, as we delve into their stories, we discover oh so many ways our lives mimic theirs. Their daily struggles, coupled with their roads to redemption, guide us as we navigate our own paths toward eternity with the Heavenly Father.

One passage that will have an impact on this study is 2 Timothy 3:16-17:

"All Scripture is God-breathed and is useful for teaching, rebuking, correcting and training in righteousness so that the servant of God may be thoroughly equipped for every good work" (NIV).

Have you ever reshaped this verse into a beautiful daydream? Imagine it along with me. Visualize our Heavenly Father, *the Great I Am*, sitting on His throne. He leans down and exhales His holy breath over those He chose to record His Scripture. That powerful exhale coming from His lungs, transformed simple words, phrases, and sentences into Truth that is living, active, and sharper than a sword. And guess what? All of this was done for you and for me, right here, right now, in whatever situation we find ourselves. It teaches us. It scolds us. It corrects us. It strengthens us to do God's glorious work.

Did you know the breath used by God to inspire Scripture is the same powerful breath He used in Genesis 2:7 when He leaned over His newly created earth and breathed life into the lungs of His precious, beloved human. Yes, the powerful breath of God is the maker of all life. He breathed spiritual life into His Word and physical life into His creation of mankind.

In my effort to be truthful and transparent, I must admit there is much I do not know about God. However, this one thing I know to be true: When God said in 2 Timothy, **ALL** Scripture is God-breathed (inspired), God meant **ALL**. No exceptions. The impact of **ALL** Scripture being inspired means every story recorded on the pages of Scripture, even the most bizarre ones, are included with purpose. Think about the story of Balaam's talking donkey. Perhaps that weird yappy-donkey story was God's way of saying if He can use the mouth of a donkey to speak His truth, He can certainly use our mouths, too. Perhaps God is saying it's time for all Christians to speak up!

Now you might be wondering why this book is entitled, *Untying Yesterday's Knots*? Although biblical heroes of old were instruments of God's plan, they certainly had their faults. In fact, they failed miserably at times. Our tendency is to immediately shake our heads in shame and judge their shortcomings. What we will discover is the same mistakes made long ago still have a way of tripping us up today. In fact, we can do a holy face-plant if we aren't careful, just as if our shoelaces were knotted together. And perhaps we tripped and stumbled over their same mistakes yesterday.

As we make our way through this book, we should ask ourselves, *What does this story teach me about our Heavenly Father?* and *How will this story draw me closer to the heart of Jesus?* If we do, we must not be surprised when we are called to make changes in our lives. That is what inspired Scripture is designed to do as it speaks goodness, grace, and truth to us.

So, are you ready to inhale some incredible stories straight from the breath of God and allow their sweet aroma to fully equip us for His good work? Today promises to bring its fair share of challenges, and we certainly do not want to trip up in the same ways those of faith did long ago. So friend, reach down, unknot those laces, and let's take off.

Blessings,
Rita

Grateful Recognitions

To my husband who has faithfully supported and encouraged me all along this book-writing journey, even though he must still be reeling from the challenges and tears of my first book.

To my six grandsons who give me every reason to be proud, yet in their own unique ways, keep me humble by reminding this control-freak that God alone is in control.

Most importantly, to my Heavenly Father, who covers me daily with His grace and loves me unconditionally with His mercy, even though I am far from being found worthy.

"All Scripture is God-breathed and is useful for teaching, rebuking, correcting and training in righteousness so that the servant of God may be thoroughly equipped for every good work" (2 Timothy 3:16-17, NIV).

The Knotted-Up Life of Eve

Untangling the "Wants" in Our Lives

Friend, here we are, ready to jump into someone else's life. The curiosity in me is excited about this! Now if I were to tell you the woman whose life we are about to confiscate is legendary, you might think she was perfect and that she resides on a pedestal today. But, oh, that is quite far from the truth.

This exceptional woman was Eve, and her journey took her from a world of paradise to a world of pain. Perhaps it would be advisable for us to begin this study in prayer, asking God to give us eyes to see and hearts to follow the path He desires for us as we study this matriarch. Write your prayer on this chapter's notes page.

Now that we are fueled by prayer, let's stop and read Genesis 3. Record any first thoughts or questions you may have. Then, as you go through this study, look for the answers from Scripture.

In this single chapter, God's perfect creation fell from a mountaintop into the deepest valley. Adam and Eve moved from a peaceful life to a painful life. We must not overlook this difficult chapter because, remember, the rocky paths of those found in Scripture will help us avoid the same mistakes.

Let's consider what actions caused Eve to fall away from her life of perfection.

1) Eve granted an audience with the evil one.

I have no clue what you wrote as your first thoughts of Genesis 3, but the first question I had was about this serpent. What a strange and frightful encounter! Yet there is no indication Eve was frightened. Perhaps this can be explained by the description of this serpent given in verse 1. "Now the serpent was more _____ than any of the wild animals."

Now, we must know that being cunning, or subtle, or crafty is not inherently evil. These traits can be positive in nature. However, this evil serpent did what he did best: He took what was good and used it for evil. His cunning and crafty nature gained Eve's trust in a way that dispelled all her fear. I still find that amazing, because at the first glance of any serpent, and I do mean any, I resort to flight-mode!

Consider how we can use what is good for the purpose of evil. What other human traits can we use for both good and evil? Explain.

_____

If only Eve had realized who the serpent was. His identity is made clear to us in Revelation 12:9: *"So the great dragon was cast out, that serpent of old, called the Devil and Satan, who deceives the whole world"* (NKJV). Yikes, did you just notice the word deceives is in present tense? Beware, for that Devil, yes Satan, is still deceiving us today!

This cunning serpent was quickly granted an audience with Eve, allowing him to strike up a conversation. His words in verse 1 comprise the first recorded question in the history of the world. *"Did God really say, 'You must not eat from any tree in the garden'?"* (NIV) the serpent asked.

Have you ever considered why the serpent's first words to Eve were in the form of a question? He could have just made a statement like, "God never said you could not eat of every tree," because one of Satan's greatest talents is lying! So, why a question? Record your thoughts, then I will share mine.

Don't questions require us to stop, process, and then verbalize our thoughts? Questions require a greater investment into the conversation whereas statements require no further response. The serpent simply planted a seed of doubt with his question, knowing Eve would continue to mull it over in her mind (as my Gran would have said) and stick around to respond.

What Satan planted that day was a seed of doubt surrounding God's deity. His words were intentional and tactical, even down to the word, *indeed* or *really*. Did God *really* say this?

Years ago, I witnessed a crime. Because I was the only eyewitness, the police grilled me with questions. Before meeting with the authorities, I was positive about what I had seen. But as they questioned me with, "Did you really get a good look at him?" and "Are you sure of what you saw?" they planted seeds of doubt, and by the end of that interview, I was not even sure I had witnessed a crime at all.

The same happened to Eve. Satan's seed of doubt led Eve to question everything she knew to be the truth about God. When Eve questioned truth, she willingly took a bite of what was forbidden. With that one simple choice, her perfect garden life ended, and our world changed forever.

That cunning devil! What does God's Word tell us to do with the crafty devil in James 4:7?

When Eve questioned truth, she willingly took a bite of what was forbidden.

Brainstorm some solid ways you plan to resist and flee.

2) Eve wanted what she could not have.

"So when the woman saw that the tree was good for food, that it was pleasant to the eyes, and a tree desirable to make one wise, she took of its fruit and ate. She also gave to her husband with her, and he ate" (Genesis 3:6, NKJV).

Satan had Eve's full attention, so he carefully chose his next move. He appealed to her on a more sensual level and dangled in front of her what looked and felt good.

- Satan convinced Eve the fruit tasted good—(lust of the flesh).

- Satan showed Eve the tree was pleasant to look at—(lust of the eyes).

- Satan assured Eve the fruit would make her wise like God—(pride of life).

Every move Satan makes is intentional. In fact, Scripture warns us of his tactic in 1 John 2:16. John says the following are of the world and not of God: the lust of the flesh, the lust of the eyes, and the pride of life. Look back above, and you will see all three of these represented in Satan's conversation with Eve. Satan uses this tactic again, many years later in Matthew 4, with Jesus in the wilderness. Sadly, Eve fell for it. Gratefully, Jesus resisted it.

Turn back to 1 John 2:16 and consider what appeals to our senses: our flesh, our sight, and our pride. These are from the world, not from God, yet we, humans, are drawn to them like magnets. What are some earthly things after which humans can lust or feel pride?

3) Eve surrendered to her desires.

Eve lived the good life. Perhaps her days with Adam were spent carefree in each other's company, frolicking with their animal friends, arranging lovely garden bouquets, and enjoying an intimate relationship with God.

Yes, Eve had it all—all, that is, but one special tree in the middle of their garden. It must have been an exquisite tree and certainly unique from all others because it was off-limits by God's decree. She was not to eat from it. She was not to touch it. No exceptions! But Eve desired the one thing she could not have.

Does this in any way sound familiar? When we desire what we do not have, are we not known to utter the words, "I wish?" While getting coffee recently, I overheard a woman say to the lady next to her, "I wish I was your shape." As I eyed both women, I found no fault in either of them. Both seemed perfect, yet her desire to have what she did not have is common among us. When we focus only on what we lack, we blind ourselves to all we have been given.

Do you remember a man named Achan? Joshua 7 tells of this greedy man who saw the beauty (lust of the eyes) of the gold and silver items in the Lord's treasury. He coveted them (the pride of life), took them, and hid them under his tent. Obviously, he had no genuine need of them because he rendered them useless to him the moment he buried them in the dirt. So why did he take them? It was the same as it was with Eve: Achan wanted what he could not have.

Eve desired the one thing she could not have.

None of us have been given it all, but each of us has been gifted something. On this chapter's notes page, record any talents and opportunities you possess but might be overlooking as you chase the ones you do not have. Then consider how you could be using those talents you have been given.

4) Eve's sinful shame led her to hide from God

When Eve swallowed the forbidden fruit, a new and unwelcome emotion swept over her. She felt awkward and embarrassed before God. And, not knowing how to handle this shame, she and Adam covered themselves in leaves and searched for a hiding place. (May I just interject how uncomfortable scratchy leaves must have been!)

It was here God asked His first recorded question. "Where are you?" Remember, God already knew where they were. His question was designed to engage Adam and Eve in a conversation about their sin and bring them out of hiding.

Does hiding from God work ever work? Think about others in Scripture who tried it and were also unsuccessful.

- Gideon, in Judges 6:11-12, hid out of fear, but God found him and strengthened him for leadership.

- David, in 2 Samuel 11, hid his sin before God and the nation, but God revealed it and redeemed him.

- Jonah, in Jonah 2:2, ran away to hide from God's calling, but God met him in the belly of the great fish and redirected his life.

- Ananias and Sapphira in Acts 5:4 tried to hide the truth, but God revealed their hidden secret and exposed their greed.

Hebrews 4:13 gives us valuable information about God's eye. In your own words, what does it tell us?

5) God's love for Eve never failed, even in her sinful state.

We must not put this story to rest here, or we'll miss the best part. You see, although God's beloved creation had sinned, God was ready to show them the depth of His great faithfulness. He lovingly fashioned animal-skin tunics for Adam and Eve before they walked out of the garden forever. (Who could have guessed God would be the first fashion designer?)

Have you ever considered the magnitude of this simple act? Yes, there would be consequences for sin, but God's first move was an intensely personal one as He provided comfortable clothing for His beloved. It is of vital importance to notice the origin of their clothing. To cover the shame of their nakedness, yes, a shame born from their sin, God fashioned their clothing from animal skins. Their shame-covering came at a price. Animals shed their blood so that Adam and Eve could find relief from the guilt of their sin.

Could our lives get tangled up in the same?

Oh, how critical we can be of Eve! *Why would Eve listen to such lies?*, we wonder. *How could Eve have fallen for the serpent's tactics?*, we say. But if we examine ourselves, we will see how we, too, have sinned in the same ways. We overlook truth to follow lies. We allow Satan an audience, and we fall prey to his cunning nature. We overlook everything we already possess in pursuit of what we do not have. From Eve's first sin in the garden to all the shameful sins we have yet to commit, a blood sacrifice is required. Yet, although our sins nailed the Son of God to the cross, somehow God's love for us remains steadfast. You might just want to take a moment for a well-deserved praise break!

The relevance of Eve's story is undeniable, and it is important for us to know what Scripture says about our sin and God's redemption. Write in your own words what the following verses tell you. Prepare to be amazed!

Ephesians 1:7

Hebrews 9:22

I dare you to discover anything more amazing or thought-provoking today!

6) With Sin Comes Consequences

We don't think of the serpent as being a farmer, but I can assure you he planted a seed of doubt in Eve. He buried it deep within Eve's thoughts, and he watered it with questions that invested her in his scheme. How ironic when we consider Adam's consequence for his sin was to become a farmer whose seeds would not so easily take root! And Eve's consequences brought pain in childbirth for all generations to come. Never forget, in spite of God's constant love, sin delivers consequences of the worst sort.

Tying Up the Story of Eve

It is no secret that our Heavenly Father desires our devotion, and with it, our obedience. John 14:15 says, *"If you love me, keep my commands"* (NIV). As we walk through the life of Eve, we see her intimate relationship with God and her love for Him, yet she still chose to set aside His commandments.

Perhaps we have also allowed the same scenario in our lives. Gratefully, the same loving Father who fashioned comfortable clothing for sinful Adam and Eve is our Father, too. And His love for us remains no matter our actions. As we reach out to Him for forgiveness, He is quick to redeem us. After reading 1 John 1:9, record on this chapter's notes page how this truth speaks to you right now? Stop for a pray/ petition break over what you just recorded.

Our look at Eve began with the God-question, "Where are you?" as she attempted to hide from God. Have we considered that God still asks this same question of us today? Write your name in the blank.

"Where are you, _____?

Are you trying to hide…

- from God's love and mercy?

- your talents from God instead of using them to His glory?

- from opportunities to share God's story of love and redemption with those who do not know Him?

Settle in with a cup of tea as we put this story to bed.

My early life played out as a middle school geography teacher. (Ah, the stories I could tell!) Each day's goal was to do whatever necessary for grabbing my students' attention. One successful strategy was bringing influential people into my classroom as guest speakers.

However, this was no simple task.

With our Canadian unit approaching, I began pursuing a popular local hockey player who grew up in the northern province of Nunavut. Our class orchestrated a campaign to invite him as a guest speaker to enlighten us on his culture. We sent letters. We made posters and held them up at the games. We created birthday cards. We sent Christmas cards. We emailed congratulations when he scored a goal. We did everything short of stalking him. But sadly, after all our efforts, we did not receive the first response! (In full disclosure, he did once flip a puck into the stands to my student holding up our invitation sign.)

That class graduated, and our campaign began anew the following year. Adopting a new strategy, while on our St. Louis field trip, I took a photo of our students from high in the arch. The entire class lay on the ground below the arch in the formation of this player's number: #22. We framed that photo and had it delivered to him along with our 795th invitation to come to our school!

BINGO! After an exhaustive two-year campaign, we succeeded.

As we celebrated the victory, something dawned on me. Just that morning, I had enjoyed a one-on-one intimate time with God. Yes God, the Creator of the universe, the Father of all living things, The Great I Am whose very name means unfathomable love, had met with little-old-me simply because He desired time with me. I did not chase Him. I did not vie for His attention. He did not put me off. He did not shun me because I was sinful. I simply approached His throne and entered His precious fellowship.

At any time we wish, we may approach God's glorious throne and discover Him there.

We must never forget what a privilege it is to go before the throne of God. Our Heavenly Father awaits us. Even though we, at times, allow Satan to draw us away from God just as did Eve, God still adores us. We are never an inconvenience nor an obligation to Him. Psalm 145:18 tells us, *"The Lord is near to all who call on Him, to all who call on Him in truth."*

Friends, we are never out of God's sight. At any time we wish, we may approach God's glorious throne and discover Him there.

As we conclude, record on the notes page any final thoughts or discoveries you have on Eve.

Notes

Father God, help us realize the redemption from our sins has come at a great price. Thank You for the gift of Your Son's blood.

The Knotted-Up Life
of Hagar
Untangling Our Self-Doubts

For just a moment, think back to your childhood. Did you ever attempt to run away from home? I assume you had to dive deep into your childhood memories to answer this, but in full disclosure, I will admit to having this passing thought more recently than childhood—as an exhausted mother of two toddler boys.

If you ever succeeded in making a juvenile-jailbreak, why were you running and where were you going? My personal memory was of my eight-year-old self, running from the injustice of cleaning my messy room. However, I recall it all fell apart when I reached the curb and remembered I was not allowed to cross the street. So, I was forced to go back inside, unpack the stuffed animals and saltine crackers from my little bag, and finish cleaning my messy room.

Perhaps you remember the heartache, the rage, and the fright of running away. If so, you might relate to Hagar. Her story is tangled up in all these emotions and more. But as we walk her troubled path, we may discover our lives are messy in the same way. Before we begin, pray for God to open your eyes to how you can be drawn closer to Him through Hagar's story. Write that prayer on this chapter's notes page.

An Introduction to Hagar so Subtle We Almost Miss It

Prior to any mention of the maidservant, Hagar, we find an ever-so-slight, possible reference to her in Genesis 12. Take a moment to read Genesis 12, and make any notes of interest on the notes page. Jot down any mention you may find of Hagar.

The famine caused Abram and his wife, Sarai (who will later be renamed as Abraham and Sarah), along with their nephew Lot, to travel to Egypt with all their possessions. However, in Egypt, Abram feared Sarai's beauty might get him killed, so they schemed to tell Pharoah a half-truth, making him think Sarai was his sister instead of his wife. As Abram expected, Pharoah found Sarai attractive, so the king lavished gifts upon Abram in exchange for bringing Sarai to the palace. But when the Lord plagued Pharoah's household because of it, the truth became evident, and Pharoah abolished Abram and Sarai.

It is possible we uncover the first references to Hagar in verses 16 and 20. Did you find them? Read these two verses from Genesis 12. What might the references to Hagar be?

_____

Although we do not know for sure, it is most likely the servant girl, Hagar, was one of the gifts acquired by Sarai in Egypt. You might have noticed verse 16 mentions "female servants" and verse 20 tells us Pharoah ordered Abram to leave with "all" he had. Most likely, Hagar was a part of "all" the "female servants" that left Egypt with them. Because Hagar was considered property, she would have been forced to leave her family, depart her country, and begin a new life as the handmaiden of Sarai.

If this is how it happened, (and by most all historical accounts it is), what emotions might Hagar have experienced in the aftermath of verse 20? Is your heart already breaking for her?

_____

God's Covenant with Abram Is Important to Hagar's Story

Before we dive deeper into Hagar's story, we need to investigate the promise God made to Abram because it directly affected Hagar. God's promise, spoken first in Genesis 12:1-2, was for Abraham and Sarah to birth His nation. The fact they had no children and were too old to produce an heir made God's promise difficult for them to fathom. In fact, in Genesis 15, Abram assumed his heir would be Eliezer, the patriarch head of his household. God reassured Abram the heir would "come from your own body." Now if you were Sarai, who was well past child-bearing age, and your husband had just dropped this bomb of information on you, what obvious questions might go through your head? To believe this absurdity, what must Abram and Sarai have? For a hint, read Proverbs 3:5-6, and write your thoughts below.

These verses warn us never to lean on our own understanding. Any human understanding would speak to the impossibility of Abram and Sarai's conceiving an heir at the ages of 100 and 90 respectively. But we must remember God's power to do the impossible. What a great passage of Scripture is Proverbs 3:5-6! When life gets crazy and out of control, as it often does, we can look past our own understanding and acknowledge God has the power to provide the answer.

We must remember God's power to do the impossible.

Hagar Simply Existed

If possible, read Genesis 16, and record any first thoughts or questions on this chapter's notes page.

I should have warned you to brace yourself, for there is some undeniable girl-drama going on here. To summarize the mess, a barren Sarai convinced Abram to take her maidservant, Hagar, as a second wife so that the promised heir could be born on her behalf. What an unfortunate story! Without a doubt, we can see a thousand ways for this to go wrong. But right now, let's notice a few things we do NOT see happening in chapter 16.

We DO NOT See:

- **Prayer**—Asking Abram to take a second wife was a big deal, but does Scripture record Sarai pouring out her heart to God over this monumental decision? Hagar's life was to be greatly affected by Sarai's omission of prayer. Do our selfish decisions affect others? Record your thoughts on this after reading Jeremiah 29:12-13.

- **Trust**—Abram and Sarai lacked trust and could not see how God would carry out His promise to them. So, they ran ahead of Him and set in motion a series of unfortunate events. Before we shake our heads in disbelief, aren't we, too, known to take matters into our own hands and fail to trust our Heavenly Father with our messes? Describe ways we have run ahead of God. What can we learn about God's timing from Psalm 27:14?

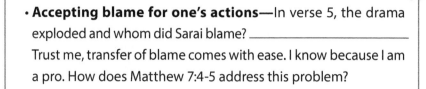

- **Accepting blame for one's actions**—In verse 5, the drama exploded and whom did Sarai blame? _____
  Trust me, transfer of blame comes with ease. I know because I am a pro. How does Matthew 7:4-5 address this problem?

- **Respect**—Hagar was Abram's wife and should have been addressed with respect. She had a name. However, notice chapter 16, verses 2, 5, and 6. How do both Abram and Sarai reference Hagar?

It seems Abram and Sarai addressed Hagar only by her demeaning title, "maid," so it is no surprise pregnant Hagar despised her mistress. Hagar reciprocated Sarai's inexcusable behavior and made her mistress's life miserable. Then Sarai retaliated with harsh treatment against Hagar. Whew! Do you have whiplash from watching this back-and-forth vengeance?

Stop to consider that Sarai claimed to be a woman of God. Hagar was raised Egyptian, and most likely held a "polytheistic" belief in many gods. While being treated harshly by her mistress, do you think Hagar could see God's spirit living in Sarai? How could this harsh treatment ever lead Hagar to desire to follow Sarai's God?

As we search for applications to our own faith walk, we must realize our lives can involve all the same struggles. My mother used to say, "If you don't do anything else, you can always serve as a bad example." At this point in the story, Sarai serves as an example of what not to do. Remember, someone out there today may be watching us to see what being a Christian looks like. How do you want them to see you today? Whom do you want them to see in you?

Hagar Flees

With no one to turn to and no one to advocate for her, not even her husband, Abram, a pregnant Hagar ran away. Look back at Genesis 16:6-13. Record any thoughts you have on this passage on the notes page.

Here is a summary of these verses before we break them down:

- Hagar ran to the wilderness.

- An Angel of the Lord appeared to Hagar.

- The Angel told Hagar to return to her mistress.

- The Angel named her unborn son, Ishmael, and prophesied his legacy.

Hagar ran to the wilderness. Perhaps she searched for a sanctuary free from harsh words and cruel demands. She needed solitude in her sorrow. Could life get much worse for this young girl?

What's in a Name?

One of the amazing things about our God is that when we are at our lowest, our God is at His best! So as fearful, pregnant Hagar sat in the wilderness pondering her next move, an Angel of the Lord appeared. The angel's first word to her was intentional. It was her name, "Hagar." I wonder how long it had been since anyone had called this woman by name. Interestingly, most always in Scripture, the first words out of an angel's mouth are, "Do not be afraid." Perhaps the angel did not need to say those words to Hagar because he knew the simple mention of her name would signify he came in peace.

When we are at our lowest, our God is at His best!

Look back at Genesis 16:9. This angel instructed Hagar to do two things. What were these and how do you think she, in that moment, felt about his requests?

What a tall ask from this bold angel! Gratefully before Hagar had a chance to protest, he continued with an unexpected prophecy of the great nation that would rise from her son. Then the angel assigned her son something precious: a name. Her child would have a name. It would be Ishmael, meaning "God will hear."

What the angel did that day was precious. God's angel offered Hagar hope for a future, something she had never felt she had. Being Egyptian, Hagar grew up with many gods, all of whom had names. In response to His gift of hope, Hagar wanted to give this loving God a gift, but she had none, so Hagar offered the only gift she had: a name. Hagar named Him, "The God who sees," because for the first time, this invisible girl felt seen.

An interesting and sad fact is that Abram and Sarai are never recorded in Scripture as having called Hagar by name. I once heard that a person's name is the most precious word in any language. Poor Hagar lacked hearing that in her life. What a blessing this girl, who by all practical purposes had no name, came into the presence of a God who knew her name, saw her pain, heard her cry, and offered her hope.

What about our tangled-up lives?

Let's consider our own lives. Do we ever feel invisible to God? I recall my brother, who during a terrible season of his life, jokingly announced, "Just give me a boil and call me Job!" Indeed, life can dish out seasons that arrive without warning and turn everything into a big dose of terrible. We can struggle to make sense of it all. Perhaps now is a good time to stop and praise a loving Father who sees us and knows our names.

How do the following "God Sees Us" verses speak to you?

Psalm 33:18	Jeremiah 23:23-24	1 Peter 3:12

The Rest of Hagar's Story

Friend, there is much more to this woman's story than we have time to tell. However, you should know, life with Sarai remained difficult for Hagar, in fact, so difficult she ran away a second time. Once again, God heard Hagar and her son, Ishmael, and as we have come to expect, God's hope-filled promise came true. Ishmael became the father of a great nation. You can read all about it in Genesis 21.

What does Hagar's story tell us about God?

Second Timothy 3:16 says all Scripture is for our benefit, so of what benefit to us is Hagar's story? Here are a few to get you started.

- With God all things are possible (Matthew 19:26)

- God uses ordinary people to do His extraordinary work, and that includes you and me!

- God can turn our tragedies into His triumphs.

- God's grace is sufficient for us.

- God sees and hears the wounded, the brokenhearted, the outcast, and the hopeless.

What other attributes of God did you discover through Hagar's story?

For the Overachiever:

Other women in Scripture also felt invisible. Their stories reiterate what Hagar came to know: God saw them. God heard them. God's love offered them hope. Here are two of them.

- The woman with a flow of blood—Luke 8:40-48

- The woman who washed the feet of Jesus—Luke 7:36-50

Story Time to Finish Up the Life of Hagar

There was no use trying to make sense of what I was hearing because my ears could decipher only total chaos. The inhabitants of this remote Guatemalan mountain village had gathered with us under a tree to pray. However, what happened next took me by surprise. In accordance with Guatemalan custom, all of them, and I mean everyone, began praying aloud their own personal prayers simultaneously. Their numerous voices blended into one deafening noise and drowned out my ability to focus. Some prayed tearfully; others prayed joyfully. Some prayed somber prayers; some shook the leaves with their shouts of praise. Some had heads bowed low; others stood with faces up and arms lifted high. The seeming disarray of it all left me a bit rattled.

As I hiked back down that steep mountain, I began reflecting on the pandemonium of their prayer, and I recalled something precious about God. What I viewed as chaos and confusion, God welcomed as praise. The village petitions mingled in an undecipherable clamor to my ears, but to the Father, it was a sweet symphony. He alone could hear every word. He alone could make sense of it all. He alone found beauty in bedlam.

Amazingly, regardless of what we confess, His love forever remains constant and steadfast.

Whenever I read Psalm 66, I smile at the memory of standing under that Guatemalan prayer tree and wonder if by any chance the psalmist ever experienced that method of prayer. The psalmist wrote, *"I cried to him with my mouth, and high praise was on my tongue. If I had cherished iniquity in my heart, the Lord would not have listened. But truly God has listened; he has attended to the voice of my prayer. Blessed be God, because he has not rejected my prayer or removed his steadfast love from me!"* (17-20, ESV).

Psalm 66 wants us to know God hears all our different prayers. He hears the cries coming from hearts filled with pain. He listens to the high praise of those whose voices shout to heaven. He understands our petitions and grieves over our pain. After we pray, we are assured, *"He has attended to the voice of my prayer."* Amazingly, regardless of what we confess, His love forever remains constant and steadfast.

Sometimes when I pray, I miss that chaos of voices, but smile just a bit knowing the Father who hears me is the same God who listens above the trees in the mountains of Guatemala and the same Father who heard Hagar all those many years ago.

Notes

Father God, we stand in awe knowing You hear our prayers from all over the world. Thank you for knowing our name as you hear our petitions.

The Knotted-Up Lives
of Joseph's Brothers

Untangling Jealousy and Envy

I am going to spill the beans right up front and tell you this week's study is all about jealousy and envy. Yikes! And why did I say, "Yikes"? Because I own those sins! It is immensely easier for me to write about the "big sins" other people commit. Their evil is clear and easy to condemn. But envy and jealousy? Often, envy just shows up and greets my morning as I scroll through social media. And sometimes, jealousy gets comfortable enough to hang around all day long. So, friend, be warned—God will call us to make some serious heart changes this week, and we might find it most uncomfortable.

If you are brave enough to join me in tackling jealousy and envy, we should stop and pray ourselves into the study. Ask the Heavenly Father to reveal our roots of jealousy and to help us rid our hearts of envy. I plan to write my prayer on the notes page, so I can circle back to it every day this week. I hope you will, too.

What is jealousy? What is envy?

Jealousy and envy are so closely related, we tend to use the words synonymously. Before we go any further, it might do well for us to first research and write their definitions.

Jealousy is:

Envy is:

You may have discovered these relate to a deep desire to have what you do not have yet someone else does. Perhaps your definition contained words like, *resentment, hostility, or bitterness*. These symptoms of jealousy and envy can be all-consuming when we allow them to take up residency in our hearts.

Let's reflect a bit: Think of an instance when you were jealous of someone or envious of something they had and you did not have. What emotions did jealousy bring out? How did envy affect your actions? Were bitterness or resentment involved? Think hard, and be honest with yourself.

It is generally thought that the most important carvings on a totem pole reside at the bottom where they are most visible to all. If sins were carved into a totem pole, those we consider "lesser sins," like jealousy and envy, would most likely be toward the top and barely visible. Hardcore sins such as murder, adultery, and thievery would be carved at the bottom and visible to all. However, as we journey through Jacob's family, jealousy's power to destroy will become evident and perhaps require us to rethink where it should reside on that totem pole.

Jealousy has earned the nickname, "the green-eyed monster." That devious title was penned long ago by William Shakespeare in his famous tragedy, *Othello*. General Othello fell under a powerful spell of jealousy. He was warned to beware of this vice, for it was a green-eyed monster that would eat him up and drive him mad. If you recall his story, that was exactly how the tragedy ended.

We also need to know right up front that jealousy and envy refuse to sit idly. They can quickly take up residence in our souls, destroy our heart health, dictate our actions, and weaken us for God's purpose. For this reason, it might do us well to walk through the tangled-up life of Jacob's dysfunctional family and see how jealousy and envy possess the power to tear families apart and drive a wedge in our friendships.

Jump on into **Genesis 37,** but be warned, we are about to witness these vices on steroids. As you read this chapter, record your thoughts on this chapter's notes page.

Jacob Bred Jealousy and Envy in His Family

More than likely, numerous character flaws jumped off the page of chapter 37. Perhaps you discovered a father who showed favoritism, a favorite son who showed a tremendous lack of common sense, and a whole passel of brothers who were fed up with it all! Let's begin with Jacob, the father.

Foolishly, Jacob made no attempts to conceal his extraordinary love for Joseph. How did you see Jacob blatantly display his favoritism of Joseph and how did this affect the rest of Jacob's sons?

Reflection time: Are we ever guilty of displaying blatant and hurtful partiality within the church, the workplace, or our community? Do we elevate some to the exclusion of others? Scripture speaks of the dangers of showing partiality. Record your thoughts on James 2:1-13.

James connects favoritism to judging. Favoritism requires us to self-rank others as we decide for ourselves how their importance stacks up against another. This ranking system requires judgments on our part. And upon what do we base these judgments? James says it comes from outward appearances and worldly material things. Both are external measures, seen through our eyes. But, when Samuel used his eyes as he attempted to pick Israel's king, God redirected the prophet to what was more important. Read 1 Samuel 16:7 to discover what God thinks is important.

Psalm 24:1 leads us to rethink worldly possessions. *"The earth is the LORD's, and all its fullness"* (NKJV). You read that right, friend. All we have in this world belongs to God. We are merely stewards of it for a short time.

In what ways do you see favoritism in your circles today?

By any chance did your mind revisit middle school and that infamous season of cliques? Do you recall being excluded from a sleepover? Perhaps you remembered the unspoken rule of who may or may not sit at the popular lunch table. These middle school nightmares sound so silly now, but are we guilty of its grown-up version? Does middle school favoritism morph into middle-aged favoritism?

When we make hurtful distinctions and exclusions among people, we are just as guilty as Jacob. Our God, above all, knows intimately whose talents and possessions are expansive and whose are lacking, yet He makes no distinctions among His people. All are equally precious in His sight. His precious Son died for the rich and the poor, the talented and the mediocre. All can be heirs to His inheritance.

Now, I think it is important to remind ourselves that having a set of close friends is not what James 2 is talking about. Even Jesus surrounded Himself with His closest group. However, Jesus was never known to be hurtfully exclusive in the process. Nor should we.

He makes no distinctions among His people.

Joseph's Role in Breeding Jealousy and Envy

As you read Genesis 37, take care not to overlook the part Joseph played in his family's debacle. Perhaps Joseph's youth contributed to his incredible lack of good common sense. Perhaps his father had instilled in him such a sense of entitlement, he felt confident to overshare. Remember, his father made no attempts to hide his favoritism, so why should Joseph? Whatever his reasoning, Joseph dished out a big heap of trouble.

Let's see how young Joseph fueled anger and resentment among his brothers.

Genesis 37: 2-3	Genesis 37: 5-8	Genesis 37: 9-11

Yes, young Joseph was a snarky teenager who tattled and bragged when he should have held his tongue. As a former seventh grade teacher, trust me when I say tattling and bragging are "death sentences" to inclusion in the middle school world. (And honestly, the middle-aged world, too!)

Scripture has much to say about our tongues and self-seeking glory. Read these, and then find others to record on the notes page.

"Sin is not ended by multiplying words, but the prudent hold their tongues" (Proverbs 10:19, NIV).

"May these words of my mouth and this meditation of my heart be pleasing in your sight, Lord, my Rock and my Redeemer" (Psalm 19:14).

At this point in the story, Joseph's youth is evident. Just wait. In time, we will see how an older, wiser Joseph will react.

The Brother's Role in Jealousy and Envy

Genesis 37:12-36 makes one observation that must not go unnoticed. Jealousy and envy are lead-in sins. What began in their hearts bled out into hateful actions. Record the brothers' jealous actions.

Genesis 37:23-24	Genesis 37:25	Genesis 37:26-28

Genesis 37:31-32	Genesis 37:35

These brothers felt no guilt. They did their evil deeds then sat down to eat without remorse. I wonder if they had to talk above the noise of Joseph yelling from the pit. Did they share a laugh over him between the entrée and dessert? This reminds me of the cold heart of King Xerxes and wicked Haman in the story of Esther. As soon as the proclamation was signed to annihilate all the Jews, the king and Haman simply sat down and enjoyed a drink as if nothing were wrong (Esther 3:15). Oh, how far from God we are when our wicked deeds cause us no concern!

Oh, how far from God we are when our wicked deeds cause us no concern!

The Power of Jealousy and Envy

Joseph's entire life from the pit forward was redirected by jealousy and envy. Jacob's heart was torn apart as this father greatly grieved the loss of his favorite son. The brothers lived with their horrible secret and the fear that one of them might betray their trust and tell the father. And Joseph's new life brought greater challenges—and blessings—than he could ever imagine.

Others in Scripture harbored jealousy and envy. Do you recall how jealousy consumed King Saul's thoughts and actions after David killed Goliath? Envy over Abel's sacrifice consumed Cain. And Ananias and Sapphira, jealous of the praise Barnabas received, lied about their gift to God.

How did their stories end? Well, Saul's jealousy led him to the attempted murder of David. Cain's jealousy led him to kill his brother, Abel. Lying to seek praise cost Ananias and Sapphira their lives.

Yes, these "small-ish" sins of jealousy and envy are lead-in sins of desperate proportion. If not identified and cast out of our hearts, they will grow and convince us to act upon their evil.

What about the jealousy of Joseph's brothers? If you know the rest of their story, it is almost unbelievable! Now, cozy up in a comfy chair if you can, and read Genesis 39-47. It will be worth the time! If that isn't possible right now, here is a recap:

- Joseph was sold in Egypt to Potiphar, an officer to Pharaoh, and with God's help, Joseph rose to power in Potiphar's house.

- Joseph was falsely accused of a crime by Potiphar's wife, and he spent years in prison.

- Through the providence of God, Joseph was released from prison.

- Again, Joseph rose to power, becoming second in command to Pharaoh in Egypt.

- During a famine, Joseph's brothers arrived in Egypt seeking food.

- The brothers found themselves standing before the very one whom they cast into a pit and sold into slavery many years prior.

- Once Joseph made his identity known, the brothers feared Joseph's power and his retaliation.

- In an unexpected move, Joseph forgave his brothers, and a happy reunion followed for Jacob's family.

The Unexpected Ending of an Unconventional God

Recall that snarky 17-year-old who foolishly recounted the dream of his family bowing to him. Genesis 42:6, 43:28, and 44:14 show how that dream became reality. I wonder if the brothers recalled that infamous dream as Joseph's identity was revealed and they bowed down before him. Surely, fear crept in their hearts as that dream became their nightmare!

What happened next was completely unexpected. At the beginning of this lesson, I warned you we would see jealousy and envy on steroids, and we have. But, in Genesis 45:4-15 we get to see forgiveness on steroids. Joseph acknowledges God's providence in his life, and because of it, Joseph chose to extend forgiveness in the biggest way! Take a moment to locate and ponder verses about forgiveness. Record them on the notes page for later contemplation.

We might think, *How could Joseph forgive his brothers for such a heinous crime?* Go back to Genesis 45:4-15, and count the number of references Joseph makes to God. How many did you find? _____God was in every breath of Joseph's story. Relate this to Matthew 19:26, *"With God all things are possible."* If God is in your story, anything, even ridiculous forgiveness, is possible!

How Do We Untangle Jealousy and Envy in Our Lives?

There will be those who are the recipients of the good fortune we desire. How does God expect us to respond? Romans 12:15 tells us to *"Rejoice with those who rejoice."* We are called to replace jealousy and envy with joy. We must never hold grudges nor use action or words that cause others harm. God says choose joy!

If we were to wrap up this family with a defining conclusion statement, it would be Genesis 50:19-20. Write this verse in your own words.

_____

What do we learn about God from this story?

- God is a merciful God and because His spirit resided in Joseph's heart, forgiveness was offered, and deep wounds of this family were healed.

- God's intervention comes in His own time. This meant Joseph spent years in slavery and prison when all seemed lost.

- God is active in our lives. What others mean for evil, God can use to His glory.

- God can grant any story a beautiful ending. Remember…

**With God at the helm,
the pit led Joseph to the palace.**

Have you come to the realization yet that this story is all about our great God and that Jacob's family were simply the supporting actors? God orchestrated it all in a way that fulfilled His perfect plan. I once saw a T-shirt that I debated ordering for my husband. However, it encapsulates God. It read,

I know stuff and I fix things. That's just who I am.

Yes, this crazy, mixed-up, dysfunctional family all came together in the end because of a Great God who knows it all and has the power to fix it all. That is just who God is.

Closing Up the Family of Jacob

Why don't you grab a cup of tea and settle in for a wee bit of story time?

We were normal elementary school girls who played outdoors and ate peanut butter and jelly sandwiches. We had all the world could offer and never imagined anything more.

Then one day, my sister and I received an invitation from a wealthy relative who wished to treat us to an "adventure day." She took us to museums we never knew existed, saw landscapes we had never before seen, and explored impressive historical sites. Then, in an unprecedented move, this matriarch allowed us to choose where we would eat lunch. She had but one stipulation; it must be a "fancy restaurant."

There was one problem: We had absolutely no concept of fancy restaurants. Growing up in a large family meant we barely had any knowledge of burger joints. But after much discussion, my sister and I agreed on the fanciest restaurant we knew existed: Shoney's, the Home of the Big Boy hamburger!

We had seen the Shoney's ads on television. You did not stand in line to order. You sat down and ordered from the table and remained there while a waitress brought your food. Plus, they had a to-die-for strawberry pie piled high with whipped cream.

We proudly announced our restaurant choice and were puzzled when her expression seemed disappointed. However, she graciously took us to our "fancy" restaurant where we got our picture made with the Big Boy and savored the most delicious hamburger, French fries, and strawberry pie in existence.

Never doubt we serve a great God who knows and directs the paths of those who trust in Him.

Today, our restaurant repertoire has expanded just a bit, and we laugh recalling our shallowness. Yet long ago, our simple little minds could not comprehend a restaurant with white tablecloths, or dimly lit candles, or silverware laid out on cloth napkins, for we had never witnessed such unimaginable places.

In the same way, God and His divine providence in our lives defy our comprehension. Simple human thoughts cannot think nor even imagine what lies in our future, but never doubt we serve a great God who knows and directs the paths of those who trust in Him.

Notes

Father God, help us focus on Your abundant blessings in our lives and may we never lose ourselves searching for what others have.

The Knotted-Up Lives
of Jochebed and the Midwives

Untangling Our Issues of Courage

We are inviting three incredibly brave women into our study this week whose names are Jochebed, Shiphrah, and Puah. Since these women are not considered major players in Scripture, they might be unfamiliar to you. However, their actions have earned them legendary status, in fact, so legendary that the Holy Spirit inspired their names and their stories to be recorded in Scripture for us.

Jochebed was the mother of a well-known Bible character, and Shiphrah and Puah were the midwives in her story. The hardships faced by these three will inspire us and strengthen us when we come face-to-face with the hard things in life. Long ago, God chose to weave the stories of these remarkable women into His everlasting story, knowing we would find inspiration from their courage.

Let's stop and write a prayer on this chapter's notes page. Ask God to open our eyes and our hearts to how the stories of Jochebed, Shiphrah, and Puah can empower us and fill us with courageous faith.

A Most Unconventional Birth

Before we jump into their story, let's stop to think about the birth of a baby. This event is one of life's greatest celebrations. Excitement is over-the-moon as the birthing room fills with joy, laughter, and bear-hugs of the grandest sort. The entire process is documented with video posts that immediately go viral, racking up triple-digit numbers of heart emojis. And when the new parents bring that bundle of joy home, more chicken casseroles and chocolate pies than can possibly be consumed fill the refrigerator. Keeping this in mind, read Exodus 1—2:2 and see how God uses three women and one unconventional birth to write a chapter in His story.

I hope you didn't read the passage expecting a sweet, endearing narrative. If so, you were out of luck, weren't you, for there was stress on every level! Pharoah was ill-tempered over the strength of the Israelite slaves, so he overworked them to the point of exhaustion. The Israelite women were terrified to give birth to a male baby because of Pharoah's edict of death. And the midwives were burdened with an order to carry out the king's death sentence, killing all baby boys. This story is one big heap of disaster.

The Plight of the Midwives

Let's turn our attention first to these midwives. A midwife's profession generally brings life and joy into the world. All joy vanished in the blink of an eye when Pharaoh ordered the midwives to be his instrument of death and kill all newborn males. These God-fearing women faced a monumental decision. Would they, out of fear, bow to the edict of Pharoah, or would they, out of desire, remain faithful to Jehovah God?

I have often wondered if these midwives met in secret to discuss their plight. Did they hold each other and cry over their dilemma? Did they pray fervently for guidance and strength? How did they encourage and build each other up when they came to the decision to ignore the king's edict? As they risked their lives to serve Jehovah, surely, they discussed the repercussions that would follow by ignoring mighty Pharaoh.

You may not have considered this, but friend, our own story is disguised within the debacle of the midwives. We, too, face difficult choices of where we place our allegiances. Do our decisions reflect an allegiance to God or to man? Remember, we have already referenced Joshua. Let's review his advice in Joshua 24:14-15:

- Who is responsible for making our decision of whom to serve?

- When should we make the decision of where to place our allegiance?

Do our decisions reflect an allegiance to God or to man?

Yes, we alone are responsible for our decisions and convictions. And timing is everything. We must choose where our commitment lies—and we must do that today!

All choices come with options. Do you know from what options Israel was to choose? If this were a modern-day, popular television game show, Joshua 24:15 may be written like this: "You can choose what is behind…

- **Door number one!** We can serve the gods (idols) of our **PAST**. This was the door their fathers chose as they served idols, and we can choose this door, too.
- **Door number two!** We can serve the gods (idols) of our **PRESENT**. This door will be the easiest because these idols surround us right now and are accessible to us.
- **Door number three!** We can choose to serve the true and living God. This is the God of the **FUTURE**, whose love and faithfulness to us will last throughout eternity.

Friend, there are always choices to make—choices representing our past, our present, and our future. We may need to walk away from what haunts us in our past, those things weighing us down and preventing us from serving God. Perhaps we need to release the stresses of today that fill our calendar, leaving us no time to know God. But, like the midwives and Joshua, our best choice remains in our future and serving the God of eternity.

I imagine you have heard the saying, "Don't make a mountain out of a mole hill." The reality is small mole hills quickly turn into tall mountains. Consider how our tiniest thoughts drive our actions. Our repeated actions become our habits. Our habits exhibit our character. Our character dictates our choices. Our choices determine our life's story. And our life's story establishes our eternity. So, if we consider this progression, our smallest choices are, indeed, vitally important, because yes, mole hills do eventually make tall mountains!

Recall a time you faced a major decision. Perhaps it centered around your job, or affected your social circles, or was something to which your own desires called you. What process did you use to come to a decision that honored God above all else? List scriptures that helped you arrive at your decision.

Need more courage? Check out these additional verses and write each in your own words.

Acts 5:27-29	Colossians 3:23-24

Did you know God honors godly choices? He rewarded these midwives for their courage and faithfulness by providing them with households. (Not bad for slave women.) Moreover, in a tribute of a far grander scale, God inspired the names of these slave women to be recorded on the pages of Scripture. So, there you have it! Two midwife slaves, whose names were Shiphrah and Puah, left us a legacy of faith and inspiration to do the hard things. Friend, find someone who needs courage today and share with them the story of Shiphrah and Puah. They will be blessed because you did.

Before we move on, take a moment to reflect on these brave midwives. What encouraged you from their story? Record this on the notes page.

The Plight of Jochebed

Now, on to Jochebed. Exodus 2 introduces us to a brave set of parents, Amram and Jochebed. (You should know that their names are not recorded until later in Exodus 6:20, but since I have read ahead, I thought I would share them.) Before we investigate the plight of these parents, you should be warned, their predicament placed them where no parent would ever desire to be placed. It was a good thing Jochebed trusted Jehovah in a big way, because without Him, all this momma had was possibly the worst plan ever devised. Stop and read Exodus 2:1-10 then ask yourself, *Doesn't God write the best stories?*

It isn't hard to imagine Jochebed's pregnancy consisted of midnight cravings accompanied by constant prayer, pacing, and plotting. When the big day arrived and the midwife announced Jochebed's baby to be a boy, the tears shed by these parents must have been a mixture of pure joy and intense panic. I recall giving birth to my son. A big celebration erupted as the doctor announced, "Congratulations, it's a boy!" But for poor Jochebed, there were most likely no words of congratulations uttered, and this mother's heart surely filled with frightful thoughts. How was she to save her precious baby boy? Hiding him was merely a temporary solution to her crisis because she knew from experience, babies do not remain silent for long. So, when desperate times called for desperate measures, this desperate mother executed a desperate plan, one that perhaps had been months in the making and covered with more prayer than could ever be counted. Describe Jochebed's plan found in Exodus 2:3-4 but hold on tight because it's a doozie!

Now, stop and read aloud the words you just wrote. Does it not sound like the most absurd plan you have ever heard when you verbalize it? Poor Jochebed! If floating her precious, beautiful baby boy in a makeshift basket-bed on the crocodile-infested Nile River was the best plan this desperate momma had, it is a good thing she trusted God with her story.

I cannot imagine Jochebed's heartbreak as she pitched her baby's basket with tar. Did she wet it with her tears? How many trips did she make to the water's edge searching just the right spot, testing out the little basket for leakage, and scanning the Nile for crocodiles? As she wrapped her son up tightly, kissed his sweet little brow, placed him gently in the basket, and laid him at the water's edge, what might have been the thoughts coming from this momma's heart and the words of her prayers? What would yours have been?

Are you ready to learn something most intriguing about Jochebed's crazy plan? Hebrews 11:23 reveals,

"By faith Moses, when he was born, was hidden three months by his parents, because they saw he was a beautiful child; and they were not afraid of the king's command" (NKJV).

What? "By faith" they were "not afraid"? Take a moment to let this soak in. Jochebed and Amram held no fear in their hearts. They did not consider they were placing their son in the crocodile-heavy Nile. They considered they were placing their son in the hands of Jehovah God. Their trust in God provided them courage to relinquish this baby to an unknown future that was out of *their* control, but never out of *God's* control.

As I read this, my heart skips a beat because above all other vices, I love to be in control. During my years as a middle school teacher, the survival of every day depended on one thing: Was I in control? After years of this mindset, my husband called it to my attention that this whole, "I must be in control" concept had crept into all aspects of my life and was affecting my relationships with my friends and family, not to mention with him. Yikes! What a revelation that was, but he was totally right. Relinquishing control is difficult. And, giving over control to God who has the power to right the wrongs and direct our paths requires that we build up the trust of Jochebed.

Scripture is rich with verses designed to fill us with the courage to trust God. Read Proverbs 3:5-6 (yes again) and Matthew 19:26, and record on the notes page how Jochebed lived out these scriptures.

Their trust in God provided them courage to relinquish this baby to an unknown future that was out of *their* control, but never out of *God's* control.

Jochebed trusted. God delivered. Ironically, this unconventional God took the water meant to kill Jochebed's baby and used it, instead, to save her baby. This unconventional God took an Egyptian princess with an order to kill this baby (Exodus 1:22) and wrote this princess into His story to save an entire nation of people.

Some would say this is impossible, but Jochebed's story is just one of many "impossible" God-stories found in Scripture. Here are a few other "impossible" God-stories. Read them when you have time.

- God conquered Jericho using a prostitute and a trumpet (Joshua 6).

- God conquered the Philistine nation using a boy, a slingshot, and a rock (1 Samuel 17).

- God conquered death with His breath, bringing back to life the lifeless body of Jesus (Mark 16).

Friend, when you consider these, a baby in a basket that saved a nation is nothing more than God's everyday routine. "Impossible" is what God does best!

What Does Courage Look Like in Our Lives?

Courage can be demonstrated in many ways, some great and some small. Allow me to share a true story of courage that cannot help but inspire us. His name was Nicholas Winton, and he lived a remarkable life. In 1939, as Hitler rose to power, news surfaced of Jews being carted away by Nazi Germany, never to be seen again. This atrocity led a young stockbroker named Nicholas Winton to get involved. With his limited resources, he devised a plan of transporting Jewish children from Nazi-occupied countries to safety in Britain.

Winton began his dangerous journey alone and never spoke of his heroic deeds until his wife discovered his scrapbook in their attic more than 50 years later. This long-forgotten gem recorded the names, ages, and photographs of the numerous Jewish children successfully smuggled to safety by her husband.

Soon after news of the scrapbook surfaced, numerous individuals came forward recalling how, as children, they had been placed on trains and transported to safety. They had never met the man who saved them. They never knew the man who was credited with saving 669 children from almost certain death at the hands of the Nazis. By the time Winton's story was shared, these "children" had children, grandchildren, and even great-grandchildren of their own and the number of lives credited to this one man had increased to 15,000.

Nicholas Winton's legacy is attributed to his individual initiative. Yes, group initiatives were quietly working to help the Jews and numerous underground resistance programs were in place, but Nicholas chose a different path. His heart called him to a solo journey. And, oh, what a difference this one man made.

You can live a remarkable life. You, too, can make a difference.

As Christians, we are called to save those in danger of death—spiritual death. Most likely, there are many programs in place in your local congregations reaching out to spread the gospel, feed the hungry, and assist the marginal communities. And prayerfully, we are all involved in these wonderful ministries. But, as evidenced in the life of Nicholas Winton, there is no substitution for an individual's initiative.

Are you aware it is more likely the visitor to church service is attending because they received an invitation from one individual, not because they received a flyer in their mailbox? It is more likely the visitor will return for a second visit if someone in the congregation reaches out to them personally and makes a connection. It is more likely a person will agree to sit down and study the Bible if one person encourages them, not because a Bible correspondence course arrived in their mailbox.

Many stories of individual initiatives are woven through the Bible. Abigail bravely appealed to David and rescued her entire family from death, saving numerous lives. A young servant girl spoke up on behalf of God's providence and power, influencing powerful Naaman to seek Elisha for healing. In turn, Naaman became a believer in the mighty Jehovah God. Philip taught the Good News of a risen Savior to the Eunuch who, after being baptized, returned to the continent of Africa with the gospel. Each of these stories relied on one individual.

So, good news! You don't have to wait on anyone else. Look around your church. Search your neighborhood. Scan your friends, and capitalize on the power of one. Just like Nicholas Winton, you can live a remarkable life. You, too, can make a difference.

We must close out this chapter, but there is much more to be said about these women. Although they are considered minor players in Scripture, their trust in God's protection awarded them legendary status. And what about this baby the midwives saved and Jochebed floated in her basket? We will meet him in our next chapter, and you are not going to believe who he became! And it was all because three women trusted God!

Notes

Father God, may our journey take us to a courageous faith in You that will move mountains!

The Knotted-Up Life
of Reluctantly Submissive Moses

Untangling the Trust Issues in our Lives

We are kicking off this chapter with a hard question: Have you ever felt reluctant to submit to God's will? Please don't close this book because you don't like your answer. Instead, grab your jersey and huddle up with me, for I am captain of "Team Reluctant." As we study the life of Moses, we will discover he wore our team jersey, too.

Moses' life took him from obscurity to the spotlight. That journey, however, would not come easy and would rob him of his peace and quiet. We find it all in the book of Exodus as it morphs through the seasons of Moses' life, from slavery to supremacy to shepherd to spectacular servant of God. God showered this reluctant servant in adventures of epic proportion, but only after Moses relinquished his own plans and submitted his life to Jehovah.

It is nothing short of spectacular to watch Moses stand boldly before the world's most powerful ruler. But before we get there, let's take a prayer-pause, asking God to help us see ourselves in the successes and failures of this man named Moses. Feel free to write your prayer on this chapter's notes page.

Leading Up to Moses

God chose Moses to lead His people out of Egypt and toward the Promised Land. Many years prior, Joseph had been sold into Egyptian slavery by his brothers. But when God's providence transformed

Joseph into one of the most powerful figures in Egypt, Joseph forgave the brothers who had betrayed him, and they became the founding fathers of the 12 tribes of Israel.

Years passed, and as we open the book of Exodus, many descendants of Joseph's brothers were slaves in Egypt where they "multiplied and grew exceedingly mighty." Their potential power so frightened Pharaoh that he took deadly measures to preserve his nation. Incredibly, right in the middle of this crazy time, God chose for a baby named Moses to enter His story and change the course of history. But first, this future leader would need a bit of coaxing and a whole lot of providential protection.

If you are ready to jump into the life of this reluctantly submissive servant, review Exodus 1 (you read it last week) and read Exodus 2.

The Seasons of Moses' Life
1) Moses, The Prince of Egypt

We cannot doubt God's providence in this story when we consider the chances of a baby floating in a basket, a slave girl playing spy, a paranoid king on the throne, and a princess taking an outdoor bath all converging at the same time and place. But in Exodus 2:3-10, God orchestrated exactly all this to assure a Hebrew baby would become a prince.

Imagine the privileged life Moses lived in the Egyptian palace. Everything this former slave desired was within his reach: the finest clothing, food, riches, and opportunities. What does Acts 7:22 tell us about the upbringing of Prince Moses?

But Moses' life of privilege was not to last and in Exodus 2:11-15, Scripture delivers an unexpected plot twist. Moses, aware of his Hebrew heritage, took "an eye for an eye" approach when he observed a Hebrew being beaten by an Egyptian, and Moses committed murder. Verse 12 says Moses did what just prior to murdering the Egyptian?

Moses knew his actions were wrong, and he took precautions to ensure secrecy. But when Grandfather Pharaoh heard of it, Moses' golden life ended when he fled the palace to seek refuge in the wilderness. I have often wondered if Pharaoh gave his princess daughter a stern, "I told you something like this was going to happen when you took in a Hebrew child, but you wouldn't listen!" Pretty sure I might have.

And just like that, one season ended, and another began for Moses.

2) Moses, The Contented Shepherd

Stop and read Exodus 2:15-22. In the wilderness by the well, Moses still looked very much the part of an Egyptian, but no one would have guessed at his royalty, for princes did not draw water for women. It would be this servant heart upon which Moses would rely. As Moses settled into a different life, he was no longer royalty but a husband, a father, and a shepherd. There were no servants at his call, no fancy purple robes to wear, and no gold around his neck, but he did not miss the grandeur. Look back at verse 21. How did Moses feel about his new life of anonymity?

We might say he found his "happy place" in the wilderness with the sheep. And isn't our "happy place" a sweet and contented place to be? Write in your own words the definition of contentment.

Tell of your own "happy place." Why are you happy there?

If, like Moses, you enjoy quietness, what positives can come from it? Psalm 46:10 gives a hint.

3) Moses, Called by God

Life teaches us our contented seasons are short-lived, so in Exodus 3, as Moses lived the quiet shepherd's life, a new season emerged. Without warning, and right in the middle of his everyday routine, Moses came into the presence of God, and everything changed. Encountering God that day was the last thing Moses expected, but as he stood before a bush aflame with Jehovah, Moses discovered God had grand, yet unwelcomed, plans for his life.

I smile reading Exodus 3:3, for here I discover Moses to be my kindred soul. Moses was curious (as am I) and talked to himself (as do I!) What did he say to himself in verse 3 as he inspected this bush?

To what purpose did God call Moses in Exodus 3:10.

Yes, God had his sights on an 80-year-old man who for 40 years had been a contented shepherd. Oh dear!

Without warning, and right in the middle of his everyday routine, Moses came into the presence of God, and everything changed.

4) Moses, The Reluctant

In Exodus 3—4, questions flooded Moses as he came to the realization God was calling him to lead a nation. Surely, he wondered what on his resume qualified him for such a position. Notice this: God called Moses in verse 10, but in what verse did Moses begin making excuses? _____ Wow! What a quick thinker he was. Moses immediately spit out five excuses, questioning God's good sense. Record these excuses found in Exodus 3 and 4.

1) 3:11 _____

2) 3:13 _____

3) 4:1 _____

4) 4:10 _____

5) 4:13_____

Does an underlying trust issue jump out at you? Moses verbalized with each excuse how unwilling, unworthy, unprepared, and unqualified he was for the job. Yet, an unfazed God met each excuse with one constant response:

I AM and I WILL do the impossible through you. Trust Me!

I jokingly remark that excuse-making is my "spiritual gift." When God messes with my contentment, excuses flow effortlessly and eloquently from my lips, exhibiting my unworthiness and unpreparedness along with a big helping of unwillingness.

But when we doubt ourselves, we are doubting God, for He promises His mighty power will work in us. What does Scripture tell us about God's power in us?

_____

Colossians 1:29

Consider for a moment our own fear of failure and self-doubt. Does it stem from a desire to be in control and have all the answers? Consider Joseph, Joshua, and Peter. Were they always in control? Did they have all the answers as they submitted to God? Absolutely not! But did God strengthen them for their journey? Absolutely yes! So, let us be bold today, knowing our great God will supply the power for whatever He has called us to do!

On the notes page, record the path you feel God calling you to walk. How can God's power aid you?

Now back to Moses. As Moses stood before the bush, God spoke directly into Moses' fears, giving him a refresher course on the **Great I AM** that burned within the bush.

- *I AM* was the God of Moses' PAST—(Exodus 3:6) He was the God who had led and protected his forefathers Abraham, Isaac, and Jacob with miracles and wonders.
- *I AM* was the God of Moses' PRESENT—(Exodus 3:14) He was the God burning before Moses, aflame with power. It was His voice Moses was hearing.
- *I AM* was the God of Moses' FUTURE—(Exodus 3:12) God would guide, empower, and mightily equip Moses for the work ahead.

Our great God sees us in ways we cannot even imagine.

The remainder of Moses' life was to be defined by the **Great I AM** living in him. From "herder of sheep" to "opposer of the mighty powers of Egypt," God powerfully equipped Moses for his task.

What about us? Our great God sees us in ways we cannot even imagine. It was the **Great I AM** who saw a mighty leader hidden deep within this wilderness shepherd. And likewise, it is the **Great I AM** who sees the potential deep within us. So, enjoy your normal while you have it because this same **I AM** is likely to turn your normal upside down to reveal your potential.

Many years later in the book of John, this apostle expounded on the **Great I AM** in seven statements. Record who Jesus claimed the **"I AM"** to be.

John 6:35 _____

John 8:12 _____

John 10:9 _____

John 10:11 _____

John 11:25 _____

John 14:6 _____

John 15:1 _____

Exactly who was this **Great I AM**? It sounds like He would be anything and everything Moses would need. And Friend, this **Great I AM** will be the same for us.

5) Moses, The Fearless Leader

Moses discovered in that bush a God who relentlessly pursues. After five unsuccessful excuses, with Aaron at his side, and the Rod of God in his hand, Moses departed for Egypt.

Let's step aside for a moment to consider this shepherd's rod. When Moses stepped into Egypt, no longer was he a shepherd. Moses held prince-status in the land of Egypt. Perhaps holding a scepter would have been more appropriate. Yet, as Moses stood before Pharaoh, his hands held a simple wooden stick. The rod of Moses was introduced in Exodus 4:1-5 and 17, but verse 20 described this stick differently. How so?_____

Moses was not the only transformation orchestrated by God. This stick, too, was given a new identity. It became "the rod of God!"

We must never doubt God's power to take whatever small possessions He has placed in our hands and use them mightily to His glory. So, friend, stop and consider all God has given you, no matter how meager. (Remember, Moses had a stick!) How can we use what is in our hands today to glorify the Father? I'll get you started: I have a cell phone in my hands (almost 24/7, I am ashamed to admit!) Today, I can use it to encourage someone who is lonely.

On the notes page, list what God has placed in your hands and how you can use it to His glory.

Again, back to Moses. When he placed his trust in Jehovah, he spoke boldly before Pharaoh. And guess what? Pharaoh responded just as Moses feared! (Remember his number 2 excuse in Exodus 3:13?) "Who is your Lord that I should obey his voice?" said Pharoah in Exodus 5:2. (I wonder if Moses fought the temptation to look up and say to God, "See, I told You this was gonna happen!)

However, if we stay with Moses, we see God fulfilling every promise He made. Seven promises of God are found in Exodus 6:6-8. They are appropriately contained between the bookend statements of *"I Am the Lord."*

God promised, *"I am the LORD. I will..."*

1) bring you out from under the burdens of Egypt.

2) rescue you from slavery.

3) redeem you with an outstretched arm.

4) take you as my people.

5) be your God.

6) bring you back to a land I promised you.

7) give you the land as a heritage.

"I Am the LORD," God said again in conclusion. Then God proceeded to check off every item on the list.

We must never doubt God to keep His promises!

Untangling My Own Knots in the Story of Moses

When was the last time you were smack-dab in the middle of your normal and God showed up with an unwelcomed opportunity? Did you, too, feel unworthy, unprepared, and unqualified? Have you ever been asked to host a missionary or called to write Bible study curriculum? Perhaps you were encouraged to take on an undesirable leadership role. And, maybe, like Moses, your excuses flowed in hopes God would lose interest and move on to someone else. Remember a contented shepherd named Moses and remember the great God who equipped him for his calling. Then rest assured, that same mighty God will equip you too.

If God calls you to do the hard things, He will strengthen and uphold you.

Pay attention to the following disclaimer should you choose to submit to God's callings.

- God's callings are rarely convenient. Moses was 80 years old and content with life when God called him and flipped his quiet existence upside down.

- God's callings will take you out of your comfort zone. Moses discovered herding sheep was far more comfortable than herding masses of complainers.

- God's callings will place in your life those who are way more needy than you bargained for. Moses discovered Israel filled with high-maintenance travelers who consumed his time and energies.

- If God calls you to do the hard things, He will strengthen and uphold you. Moses could not have convinced Pharaoh to release God's people without God's mighty power.

- God will equip you for His calling. God transformed Moses' simple wooden stick into "The Rod of God." This stick performed incredible feats done in the name of Yahweh. God calls us to glorify Him with whatever He has placed in our hands.

We began this lesson with a hard question, and we will end the same. What excuses roll off your tongue when you attempt to bypass God's opportunities?

Once Moses got past his reluctance and placed total confidence in Jehovah, his life turned legendary. So, there is much more about his journey. (Incredible plagues, amazing miracles, long years of leadership hardships, etc.) Someday, you must read the remainder of the story of this reluctantly submissive Moses, and through it, discover strength for your own journey with God. But for now, we must close out this lesson. So, let's wind it down with a real-life tie-in to Moses.

Finding Our Story in God's Power

As I sit to write this chapter, my world is abuzz with "Back to School" everything: Never ending "First Day of School" social media posts (my "like" finger now has a callous), new boxes of crayons, and a reestablished routine that sets most parents into a state of giddy joy.

As school opens and I drive through the 15-mile per hour school zones, I think of my mother-in-law and her favorite memory. In fact, having lived for several years with dementia, it was generally her only memory. The awareness of her past had faded, and our visits with her consisted of viewing the same photos each week where she viewed them with "new" excitement over and over again. At some point during our visit, Granny would always recount to us her most precious memory, as though we had never heard it. Allow me to share it with you as closely to her sweet words as I possibly can.

I know you don't know this, but a few years ago (I will insert, it was actually about 50 years ago) my son, Mike, was chosen to be the elementary school's crossing guard. I was so proud of him. Every morning he would put on his little crossing guard vest and pick up that crossing guard sign and take off walking to school. He thought he was so grown up. He didn't want me to walk with him to school. But I wanted to protect him, so I would let him go a little distance down the road, and then I would take off walking behind him. I never let him out of my sight. He thought he was doing his job all by himself and he never realized I was right there in case he needed me. If he had only turned around, he would have seen me. But he never thought to turn around and look for me.

Have you ever heard a more precious testimony to the love of a parent? Actually, you have. Because, as great a love as my mother-in-law had for my elementary school future-husband, we know our Heavenly Father loves us even deeper.

In the same way this loving, protective mother watched over her son, our Heavenly Father watches over us. The God who protected, empowered, and led Moses continues to protect, empower, and lead us on. So, today, friend, find peace knowing God's watchful eye upon you.

Notes

Father God, may we willingly relinquish our story to You and rely on Your great power and love to direct our path.

The Knotted-Up Life
of Naomi
Untangling Our Seasons of Bitterness

Friends, we are about to dive headfirst into the lives of two women in Scripture who shared a special bond. They were survivors of the grandest sort! Being a survivor means your triumph is celebrated only after you've walked through tragedy. Brace yourself because their story is far from a bed of roses. This mother-in-law/daughter-in-law duo known as Naomi and Ruth, together built a new life on the heels of their devastation. If you are willing to wade through their drama, I guarantee the ending will deliver a beautiful garden of hope. Through their story, you will discover endearing attributes of God. Remember to record all the godly attributes on this chapter's notes page. (And I hope you fill up the notes page!)

If possible, read the short book of Ruth. As you read these four chapters, remember to be on the lookout for God's attributes and providence.

Just to jog your memory, write the definition of the word *providence*.

_____

_____

The Crazy Ins-and-Outs of Naomi's life

Naomi's journey packs a punch from the get-go. Better hang on tightly because this is a summary of just the first six verses.

1) Famine struck Judah when God's people forsook His commandments.

2) Naomi and her family made the difficult decision to migrate to Moab.

3) Naomi's husband, Elimelech, died, and she was left to raise two sons in a foreign land.

4) Both Naomi's sons married Moabite women, but soon afterwards, both sons died.

5) Naomi found herself living in poverty with her two daughters-in-law, Orpah and Ruth.

Certainly, these events required difficult decisions from Naomi. Record your thoughts on what changes you would have to make in your life should these circumstances be yours.

_____

_____

In the book of Leviticus, God had promised His people food in abundance, and we know God cannot lie. (Hint: That's an attribute of God worth writing on the notes page) However, God's promise of abundance was linked to instructions Israel ignored. Doesn't this tell us something important about God? You can write this on the notes page too:

God always keeps His promises, but they come with important instructions.

As the book of Ruth opens, there is widespread famine. Put on your brave face and visualize Naomi cradling her sons and attempting to silence their cries of hunger. Were her lullabies enough to lull them to sleep? Did the sights of freshly dug graves and the widespread smell of death each morning fill Naomi with fear her sons might die while she slept. Oh, such painful thoughts for a mother!

Difficult times call for difficult decisions to be made and protective parents, Naomi and Elimelech, believed remaining in Judah was too great a risk. So, they gathered their belongings, said tearful good-byes to friends and family, and departed for Moab.

All parents on some level will be faced with difficult decisions as they raise children.

Let's pause and attempt to untie the difficulties of their decision. Moab was a heathen country, neither knowing nor serving Jehovah God. Their choice to leave Judah meant forfeiting their precious village of faith to protect their precious sons. They must have felt it was one or the other, but not both. Choosing to raise their boys in an ungodly nation surely agonized these parents.

Consider the pros and the cons of their decision to move to Moab. What would you have chosen to do?

We may be critical of their decision if we have never feared for our child's survival. However, all parents on some level will be faced with difficult decisions as they raise children.

I had a conversation with a young mother who had moved an hour away from our church. She agonized over the struggles of getting two small children up, dressed, fed, in the car, and arriving on time for Bible class. She mentioned a wonderful, yet small, church located minutes from their new home. The thought of leaving her beloved church family saddened her, but she feared they would not remain faithful from such a distance. As we discussed her dilemma, we concluded that this was just the first of many hard decisions she would be called to make for the good of her children. It is what parents are called to do.

If you are a parent, what are some of the difficult decisions you have made for the good of your child?

What guided your decision? List any scriptures here that helped.

Naomi's Difficult Choice

According to studies, the death of a spouse is one of life's most difficult seasons, surpassed only by the death of a child. Poor Naomi suffered both tragedies. I wonder how many tearful nights the widow Naomi lay awake calculating the risk of staying in Moab versus the risk of returning to her homeland. I hope it was through much prayer that Naomi made the decision to return to Judah.

The Daughters-in-law's Difficult Choices

Since this story revolves around a mother—and daughter-in-law, we might expect conflict since in our society, the relationship is assumed to be a difficult one. I once read the following anonymous statement about in-law relationships:

"Don't tell me how to raise my children," said the daughter-in-law to her mother-in-law. *"Obviously, I'm still raising one of yours!"*

Yikes! Gratefully, we do not find this represented in Naomi's relationship with her daughters in-law, and I pray this does not represent any of ours.

When Naomi decided to return to her people, she begged her daughters-in-law to remain in Moab with their families and a chance to remarry. Look back at Ruth 1:11-12. Naomi offered the girls no hope! How sad to be in a place of "no hope." As the girls considered the "whys" and the "what-ifs" of staying behind with family or going forward with Naomi, it made more sense for Orpah to stay behind. For Ruth, it did not.

All you mothers-in-laws out there might need to grab a tissue before you read Ruth's words to her mother-in-law in Ruth 1:16-17. From them, you get a sense of Ruth's tender heart and loyalty. Little did this young woman realize her words would gain legacy status as a testimony to everlasting love.

First Corinthians 13 is known as the New Testament's chapter on love. Compare it to what Ruth says to Naomi. What similarities do you see between the two?

Naomi's Bitterness

After hearing such sweet words from Ruth, you would think Naomi would be overwhelmed with gratitude. However, instead of feeling embraced, from verses 18 and forward, Naomi was bitter. Perhaps she felt guilt over the decision to move her family to Moab. Did she consider life might have been better had her family remained in Judah and faced the famine head-on? Whatever her thoughts, Naomi fills her heart with bitterness!

Now before we criticize her, we must admit bitterness invades our lives, too, and it doesn't look good on us either. Let's examine Naomi's journey and see if it can enlighten us to better understand and avoid its pitfalls ourselves. Here is the ugly truth about bitterness:

Consider the importance of gratitude. Who needs to hear your words of gratitude today?

1) Bitterness affects our behavior.

In Ruth 1:18, Naomi gave up trying to persuade Ruth to stay behind, and off they departed. Interestingly, Hebrew Scripture translates verse 8 as, "she (Naomi) left off speaking unto her (Ruth)." Yikes! Did Naomi stop talking to Ruth? Oh, I do hope for Ruth's sake, Naomi's silent treatment did not last the entire trip, or that must felt like the never-ending journey!

Did you notice something missing? There seem to be no words of gratitude recorded from Naomi. Surely Naomi was grateful Ruth remained with her. Sweet Ruth had forfeited everything for Naomi: her homeland, her friends, her family, and her culture. Wouldn't we expect a few niceties from Naomi, perhaps an, "I am so blessed by you, dear Ruth!" or "I don't deserve you, sweet Ruth." Nope! None of that! Despite it all, this precious daughter-in-LOVE departed with Naomi.

Consider the importance of gratitude. Who needs to hear your words of gratitude today?

_____

2) Bitterness is never confined to our own little bubble.

Ruth was not the only recipient of Naomi's bitter disposition. Read Ruth 1:19-20. When friends and family saw Naomi, they celebrated their long, lost friend. I can easily visualize laughter and hugs, and if given time, an entire potluck supper spread out on picnic tables. However, Naomi was having none of that! So, when she announced she was no longer to be called Naomi, meaning "pleasant," she sucked the happy right out of the party. Her new name was to be, "Mara," meaning "bitter." And after the way Naomi had been acting, I am sure no one objected!

3) Bitterness will blind us.

Naomi allowed bitterness to blind her to how God viewed her. She was His precious child, but she had closed her heart to His love. With her new disposition and her new name, bitter Mara blamed God for all her hardships.

Read and consider how the following Scriptures can redirect our thoughts when we become bitter.

James 1:27	Philippians 2:4

Because Naomi looked only inward at her bitterness and never outward to see the hardships others may have had, she became blinded to Ruth's goodness. In verse 21, Naomi said to those celebrating, "I went out full, and the LORD has brought me home _____."

Is this true? Did she really return home with nothing? What about Ruth? I have often wondered if Ruth were standing nearby to hear these hurtful words. Was Ruth considered nothing? It seems Naomi was too busy nursing her bitter spirit to notice her hurtful words. Had I been Ruth, I would have fought back a big ole eye roll.

(Perhaps this is a good time to stop and utter a breath-prayer.) *Father God, grant me the patience to smile when an eye roll would feel so much more satisfying!*

Get ready to write on the notes page another sighting of God's providence. Following the whole, "I came home empty" statement, Scripture records that Naomi and Ruth arrived in Judah at the beginning of barley season. This may seem insignificant. In fact, we may overlook this until we realize Ruth's legacy was directly linked to God's leading them home during harvest season. God's timing is perfect!

Only a great God can take a simple grain and create an everlasting legacy.

How important was barley to this story? Hopefully you have read the book of Ruth, but I will offer a quick summary.

- Naomi and Ruth arrived in Judah during harvest season.
- Ruth gleaned the barley fields belonging to Boaz, a devout man of God.
- Ruth married Boaz, and they named their son Obed.
- Obed was the grandfather of King David.

Tying Up Naomi's Life with Everlasting Hope

What seemed hopeless and bitter for Naomi, turned into unimaginable blessings. When her grandson was born, her friends (perhaps the same ones she scolded for calling her Naomi), finally got to celebrate with her. "There is a son born to Naomi," they cried, and this time, Naomi did not correct them about her name, because "Mara" no longer existed.

I have saved the best of God's providence for last, dear friend, because, you see, her grandson, Obed, Naomi's precious gift from God, became part of the lineage of Christ Jesus, the Savior of our world.

As Naomi took her first tearful steps out of Moab, could she have possibly fathomed all the goodness her new life would bring? Did she ever dream her blessings would bless all generations to come? Our great God guided a desperate Naomi to a place of love and grace. And remember, dear friend…

God meets our imperfections with His perfect love and grace.

None of us desire difficult seasons. Naomi's difficulties of death and famine lay beyond her control. Let's stop to examine other causes of our difficult seasons, and by doing so, perhaps we can avoid bitterness in our lives.

- Sometimes our difficulties are because of evil in this world. Remember, Jochebed, Moses' mother, feared Pharoah's evil death decree and placed her infant in a basket on the Nile River (Exodus 1-2).

- Sometimes our difficult seasons are 100 percent because of our own sinful self, as with King David who chose pride, adultery, and murder (2 Samuel 11).

- Sometimes difficulties stem from the actions of others. Abigail found herself plopped right down in the middle of someone else's mess (1 Samuel 25).

- Sometimes we allow fear to trump our faith. Peter was so frightened he denied the Christ (Luke 22).

We may overlook the presence of a loving Father who stands with us in the middle of our chaos.

God, however, met each of these imperfections with His perfect love and grace, so here is the rest of their story.

- Jochebed's basket saved, not just her baby, but an entire nation.
- David became Israel's greatest king and through his repentance, earned the title, "A man after God's own heart" (ref. 1 Samuel 13:14).
- Abigail's debacle led her to the king's palace and a queen's throne.
- Peter boldly stood and preached of a risen Savior on Pentecost.

Our paths, like Naomi's, can be burdensome and deliver us to unwelcomed destinations. An uncertain future may loom over us and cause us to focus only inward, blinding us from those who need our help to survive their battles. We may overlook the presence of a loving Father who stands with us in the middle of our chaos. The Book of Ruth reminds us God never leaves us. He will lead us through the darkness into a new day. But be warned, our journey may not be down our chosen path, and it may be incredibly more difficult than ever imagined. But rest assured, God can make the journey worth the effort.

Takeaways to Ponder

What crisis do you face today? Financial? Marriage? Children? Health? Or perhaps faith? Brainstorm how to battle life's hardships knowing God is with you. Include scriptures that will help. I will get you started, *"I can do all this through Him who gives me strength"* (Philippians 4:13), NIV.

Take time for reflection. What did you learn about our great God from Naomi and Ruth?

How can the story of these two women bring us closer to the heart of Jesus?

Settle into a comfy chair as we finish up Naomi with story time.

Several years ago, my students and I stood around comparing stories of our most memorable vacations. I held them spellbound as I recounted the story of our now infamous Cancun trip. The short of it goes like this: My husband's kidney stones flared up just as the plane took off. Paramedics were waiting for him when we landed in Atlanta where an ambulance whisked us off to the emergency room. We spent a long and painful night there and arrived a day late in Cancun. We quickly discovered our reservation at the tropical resort had been given away, and to boot, our luggage was lost. Taking pity on us, the resort issued us staff t-shirts to wear that led everyone to assume we could speak fluent Spanish when in fact, "hola" was all we had. Thinking the worst was over, two (did you hear me say TWO?) strong earthquakes hit Cancun in a single day and shut down the entire city. We were evacuated from our resort and left with nothing but vending machine options for our meals.

My students and I were enjoying some group laughter over my story when one student spoke up and said, "That's the best story I ever heard! I wish that was my story!"

I chuckled at the comment and remarked how I would never wish that story on anyone. I reminded them how each of us is drafting our own unique stories from every encounter, every decision, and every word spoken through every moment of our lives.

Same with Naomi.

God will never leave us. He will lead us and cover us with His redeeming love.

The moments comprising Naomi's story were written with much pain, hardship, and uncertainty. Perhaps your story is reminiscent of hers, and you too hold bitterness. Or perhaps your story does not yet contain chapters of difficulty. Regardless of where we live, how old we are, the color of our skin, the size of our bank account, or the logo on the jerseys we wear for playoffs, there is one amazing story belonging to us all. This beautiful and perfect story for all humanity is the story of God's redeeming love.

God never left Naomi. He led her every step of the way to her new and glorious beginning. He gave her reason to turn her bitterness into praise. Friend, never forget the real story. God will never leave us. He will lead us and cover us with His redeeming love. This great story is Our Story!

Notes

Father God, help us to look past the trials of the day to see the redeeming love You have waiting for us at the end of our journey.

The Knotted-Up Life
of a Woman Caught in Naughty Sin

Untangling Our Lives from Sin

Welcome back, friend. This week, we will look at the confusion created when Jesus encountered an adulterous woman. I'm excited about this lesson because it is one of my favorites. (Of course, I say that often, but who's counting!) There may be some question as to why it's a favorite since this account is about adultery, a sin we prefer to keep in the dark where it belongs. But, before you close your book and go in search of something happy and jolly, I want you to know, once you travel through the horrible realities of this story, you will discover the sweetest of endings.

As we walk through this woman's story in John 8, we will see the deity of Jesus tested. Because Jesus knew every detail of what lay ahead, even the Savior needed to be filled with His Father's strength and peace. So, as the curtain rises on our scene, Jesus is on the Mount of Olives, spending precious time alone with His Father.

Take a moment yourself, all alone with the Father, to prepare for the pain of having your sins revealed through a woman caught in a naughty sin. Pray to see your own naughty sins that separate you from God. Write your prayer on this chapter's notes page.

Trapped in Naughty Sin

You should know there will be nothing easy about this lesson, beginning with a difficult assignment: Think of a time you experienced unspeakable embarrassment. I mean, remember a time when you did something so terrifying, you hyperventilated, and the blood drained from your face. Recall an embarrassment you can never forget, not even if you live to be 100 years old, are diagnosed with Alzheimer's, and in a rocking chair at an assisted living facility. Think of the one memory that will haunt your nightmares the remainder of your life. And if you are brave enough, jot that memory down on the notes page. (Sadly, I had a few to remember!)

Now, prepare to witness an embarrassment so great it will make your personal embarrassment seem a tiny gnat on a giant log. The woman in our lesson today endured the unspeakable shame. Her name is never mentioned, yet John 8 records her worst day—a day when her private, most sinful act turned public. A day when her most unholy sin was drug into a most holy place. A day when her life lay in the hands of an angry mob and her sin, along with her skin, lay bare. Yes, this woman was caught in a very naughty sin, the sin of adultery.

Take a deep breath and read the first part of this unspeakable shame from John 8:1-6. Become a Scripture detective and record the *how, what, when, where,* and *why* of this account.

How did Jesus find the strength to face such a difficult day? See 8:1

What was Jesus doing at the temple? See 8:2

When did Jesus arrive at the temple? See 8:2

Where did the scribes and Pharisees place the sinful woman? See 8:3

Why did the scribes and Pharisees take an unholy woman into a holy temple? See 8:6

If Jesus relied on quiet, solitary time with God, how much more should we?

The first thing we see here is the value of beginning each day in quiet community with the Heavenly Father. Jesus was known to meet God in the quiet, solitary places. If Jesus relied on quiet, solitary time with God, how much more should we? When we come into the holy presence of God, His power will fight our battles with us. The love He gifted us at the cross will fill us with the desire to pass along grace to others. Entering His presence affords us a peace that passes so far beyond our understanding that we cannot help but stand in awe of His majesty. So, stop and brainstorm over the best time and place for you to come into the holy presence of God, because you, too, can access His strength for your most difficult days.

Next, did you see the motive of the men who took this sinful woman into the holy temple? They caught her "in the very act" of adultery. We will assume she was taken from the bed against her will and dragged into the temple wearing little clothing. It is painful to consider the shame she endured. Yes, she had broken the law and by that law was sentenced to stoning. It is worth noting what the Jewish law recorded concerning punishment for adultery. Leviticus 20:10 says,

94

"The man who commits adultery with another man's wife, he who commits adultery with his neighbor's wife, the adulterer and the adulteress, shall surely be put to death" (NKJV).

Aha! Did all you detectives just discover something overlooked by the Jews who dragged her to the temple? This sin was a tango-for-two. Where was the man? We have no answers for that, but now we do know the Jews were not concerned about the law. If so, the man would also have been dragged into the temple. No, the Jews had one purpose that day: to make Jesus seem the fool in front of the crowd.

As Jesus taught the people, a woman was hauled into the temple. Surely a hush fell over the crowd as all eyes strained to see this grand entrance. I am reminded of a time when my husband was a guest preacher for a small, rural congregation on the hottest Sunday morning on the planet. Because all windows and doors were propped open, it seemed to be an open invitation for a large, mangy dog to make a grand entrance smack-dab in the middle of his sermon. As it meandered down the center aisle, walked on the stage, and lay down right at my husband's feet, a hush fell over the church. My husband, uncomfortable about the dog's intentions, stopped mid-sentence. In the same way, the Jews that day made a grand entrance right in the middle of Jesus' teaching. Had there been a center aisle and stage where Jesus stood, this woman would have been placed there, simply for shock value. And without a doubt, an unclothed woman placed center stage would have made for a grand entrance!

Jesus Chose a Covering of Grace
Over a Pelting of Gravel

Have you ever played the game of "Finish the Story?" The first person begins sharing only a piece of a made-up story, and you move from person to person, each adding her own spin to the plot. Since I only asked you to read the first part of the passage, let's play this game together and imagine how this sinful woman's day might have gone.

On the notes page, write a possible ending that could have happened.

Perhaps you ended the story with Jesus quoting from the law of God and supporting the stoning of this woman, because, after all, Jesus claimed to be God's Son and it was God's law. Maybe you ended it with Jesus' pleading for the woman's release. This ending would have been consistent with the compassionate heart of Jesus. Or maybe you ended it with Jesus using her as an object lesson on the wages of sin, adding to her shame. Yes, any of these could be an alternate ending, but the beautiful gift of the Savior's grace would have been lost in them. Now read the real ending to this story, and discover an ending filled with grace. Read John 8:7-12.

The penalty of the law demanded her to be hit with rocks, but that day she was hit with grace—the precious grace of Jesus.

Have you ever witnessed such patience and grace? Jesus quietly stooped to write on the ground where the sinful woman sat. Perhaps Jesus had stooped beside her to share her shame and meet her in her misery (It is true, misery loves company.) But then, Jesus raised up with the proclamation,

"He who is without sin among you, let him throw a stone at her first."

The Savior, alone, could have stepped forward with a stone and wound up for the throw. But, friend, no stones were to be thrown that day. If we could hear the sounds of this story, we would hear the thuds of oh, so many stones being dropped back to the ground that day.

Aren't we glad Jesus began that day with His Heavenly Father? He desperately needed the Father's strength for what you just read. Jesus was aware that everything He said or did would go down in history and that day, Jesus chose an extraordinary Ephesians 3:20 moment. The Savior went "exceedingly, abundantly, above all" anyone could "ask or think." And so it was on that horrible day, a sinful woman stood covered in the grace of the Savior. The penalty of the law demanded her to be hit with rocks, but that day she was hit with grace—the precious grace of Jesus. I have often wondered if this woman had ever before received even the slightest gift of grace.

Right now might be a good time to remind ourselves about this thing called grace. A definition might reveal grace as the unmerited and completely unearned love and favor of God. In other words, we can, in no way, ever earn God's love and goodness toward us, but because God is love (1 John 4;8) it flows over us in great abundance.

What does Scripture tell us of God's unfathomable grace?

Ephesians 2:4-5	2 Timothy 1:9	Romans 6:14-1

Yes, Jesus was the ultimate extender of grace. During His final days on earth when Jesus endured malicious acts to both His body and His spirit, His response was not revenge, but grace.

Prepare to be amazed at the abundant grace we see Jesus extend in His final days.

- Jesus washed the feet of Judas just as He washed the other disciples' feet although He knew Judas' heart belonged to the evil one (Matthew 26:12,27).

- Jesus placed the severed ear back on the soldier who had come to arrest him (Luke 22:49).

- Jesus gifted paradise to an unworthy thief on the cross (Luke 23:43).

- Jesus said, "Father, forgive them" after they had mocked Him, beaten Him, shoved a crown of thorns upon His head, and nailed Him to a cross where He took His final breath (Luke 23:34).

- After His resurrection from the grave, Jesus welcomed back the disciples who had forsaken Him as He hung on the cross for them (Matthew 26:56).

What did grace accomplish that day at the temple? Look at verse 9. Grace convicted the conscience of each man who held a stone in his hand. Beginning with the oldest and most guilty of numerous sins and going all the way to the youngest man holding a rock, each left to lick his wounds in privacy. That's what grace does. Grace exposes our sins and convicts our hearts for what is true and honest and good.

We, too, stand in great need of grace. The shameful woman caught in the ugliest sin took one for the team that day because the truth is, she represents every ugly sin in our own lives.

This story ends in verse 12 with a seemingly unrelated "I Am" statement by Jesus. The Book of John offers us seven identity metaphors made by Jesus as He compares Himself to something tangible we can understand. One of these seven comes at the end of the story of this scandalous woman. Jesus said, *"I am the Light of the world. He who follows Me shall not walk in darkness but have the light of life."*

Take a moment and contemplate all the uses of light. Write these below.

His "I am the light of the world" statement was incredibly relevant to the situation. Consider how the deeds of adultery and the works of a prostitute are generally done under the cover of darkness. Why? Sin prefers to hide in darkness. Light is not welcome by sin, for it exposes its dirty deeds. Jesus called this woman out of her dark and sinful world when He said to her, *"Neither do I condemn you; go and sin no more."*

The light of Jesus had exposed her sin and, in the process, exposed the sinful lives of all those "righteous" ones who encircled her with stone in hand. The self-righteous accusers unknowingly lived in her same darkness, blind to their own dirty sin.

I am reminded of what Jesus spoke on the Sermon on the Mount. In Matthew 7:3-5, Jesus said, *"First, remove the plank from your own eye, and then you will see clearly to remove the speck from your brother's eye."* On the notes page, write your thoughts on what you believe Jesus meant by that.

The crowd was blinded to their sin by the planks of wood sticking out from their eyes. So, on that terrible day, they joined the sinful woman in shame as they dropped the stones from their hands and rushed home to remove the sticks from their eyes. It was a sticks and stones type of day!

I have done my best to be truthful with you throughout the pages of this book, and when I told you this tragic story would end on a sweet note, here it is. It is the gift of the precious, unmerited grace of God. Never will there be a sweeter story!

Can that be my story, too?

The Comfort Found in Grace

Go slip into some stretchy pants, get nice and comfy, and let's wind this one up with a story.

Each year, just before the New Year's countdown, I pack away the celebrations of red and green and haul off the tree. Although I'm always thrilled to reclaim my space, there is a bit of sadness as the season of merry comes to an end. With the fun, food, friends, and frivolity in the past, the time to focus on New Year's Resolutions begins.

Truth be told, I'm not a fan of it. I prefer Groundhog Day to New Year's Day because it is difficult to enjoy any holiday that comes with a homework assignment! Being that student in school who took homework seriously, I found it stressful to solidify my resolution each year on time. However, what I finally realized became a game changer: There is no one overseeing the rules for resolutions, so why not use the same resolution every year? So, I have henceforth and forevermore resolved to be like my athleisure exercise pants.

You read that correctly: athleisure pants. I hold those pants in high regard. Their value is indisputable each January when after a month of grazing, consuming, devouring, nibbling, and overindulging, those athleisure pants are the only item in my closet that continues to comfort me. These stretchy pants overlook my indiscretions of indulgence. They forgive the bulges I always regret. They sympathize with my waistline when it no longer remains as it should. They adapt to accommodate me and never gripe nor complain. They patiently wait for me to find the strength to recover from my recklessness. My exercise pants offer me grace without judgment. Perhaps if Ephesians 6 were written today, in addition to being armed with the belt of truth and the breastplate of righteousness, the armor of God would include being clothed in the grace of athleisure pants.

So now you see why each year I will resolve to imitate my stretchy pants. I will choose to offer the abundant grace Jesus offered. I will choose to forgive indiscretions. I will attempt to sympathize with the struggles of others. I will offer comfort to those hurting. And I will suspend judgment of those undergoing difficulties. The grace shown by Jesus to the woman caught in sin proved to be extravagant. But remember, the same extravagant grace is available to us when we are broken by sin.

Yes, we can find our own story in that of the woman caught in adultery. Perhaps we can be found among the crowd of those who circled the adulterous woman with stone in hand. Or maybe we can be found in the woman who sat in the dirt with her naughty sin on full display. But, friend, never forget the conclusion of our stories can be wrapped up in grace. So, if you haven't already, go right now and slip into your stretchiest pair of stretchy pants and give the good Lord thanks for this most precious gift of grace.

The grace shown by Jesus to the woman caught in sin proved to be extravagant.

Notes

Father God, there are no words for Your gift of sweet grace. May we live our lives in honor of Your grace, knowing we can never earn it.

The Knotted-Up Life
of Thomas
Untangling Our Seasons of Doubt

Oh, how I have enjoyed opening God's Word with all of you. But sadly, all good things really do come to an end. So, as we wind down our journey through some tangled-up lives found in Scripture, we will walk with one last hero: the apostle, Thomas.

Now, you might wonder how an entire lesson can be centered around a man whose story is barely found on the pages of Scripture. Three of the Gospels provide us only his name in a list, and the Book of John offers us but a smidge about Thomas. However, because his name is listed as an apostle, we know his faith in Christ was so great, he willingly put his life on hold to join the ministry.

So, this week, in place of wading through numerous chapters of Scripture, we will deeply consider a relative few verses. Through them, we will discover Thomas's legacy was built in the same way many of our legacies are built today. His legacy was built upon his weakest moment—his moment of doubt.

Allow me to confess something right here and now. As I prepared for Thomas, I was struck by how often I serve as "Hostess with the Mostest" for doubt. So, perhaps we should open this study with writing a prayer on the notes page, asking God to prepare our hearts for a deeper faith and demolish every way we doubt His goodness, His power, and His love.

Discovering Thomas

One small detail we know about Thomas was he was a twin, but his occupation, background, and family remain a mystery. It was the writer John who allowed this faithful apostle to earn his 15 minutes of fame from two short passages found in John 11 and 20. One paints him with strength and dedication to the Savior. The other reveals his questioning spirit and doubting heart.

Ok friend, did you, like me, just shake your head in disbelief? Were you considering all the spectacular events Thomas witnessed with Jesus and thinking, "How could he possibly doubt the Savior?" But you might want to take that back because what we will discover as we shake our heads at Doubting Thomas, we might be shaking them at our own seasons of doubt.

The Brave Face of Thomas

Let's begin on a positive note with John 11:1-16. On the notes page, jot down any thoughts or questions you might have as you read this passage.

Seriously, as you read the story of Lazarus, did you just think I wrote the wrong Scripture reference for Thomas? Hopefully, you stuck with the story and saw, just prior to the final curtain call, Thomas makes his brief stage appearance. Without dispute, Jesus had deep love for Lazarus and his sisters. Surely, this pulled at His heartstrings. I'm curious about the thoughts you wrote on the notes page. Did you mention that when Jesus was summoned to heal Lazarus, He dawdled? (Those are the words my grandmother might have said in her rural Tennessee tongue.) The purpose of the "dawdle" is found in verse 15. Why did Jesus delay going to Bethany?

Oh, how difficult this must have been for the Savior. He could have chosen to heal Lazarus and avoid breaking His friends' hearts. Instead, He chose to build up the faith of His apostles, including Thomas. We must remember His ultimate mission was to glorify God, and that is exactly what He did.

Now, look at John 11: 8. The apostles were opposed to Jesus' going to Bethany. John 8:59 and John 10:31 tell us why. What had happened twice in nearby Jerusalem?

I don't know about you, but I totally feel their concern. However, despite the threat, Jesus said, *"Let us go to him."* So, in John 11:16, Thomas's shining moment is seen. What did Thomas say?

Second Timothy 1:7 tells us God does not give us a spirit of fear but a spirit of power and love and self-discipline.

Two things strike me here about Thomas. First was the progression of his great faith. His faith gave birth to his bravery, and it totally dissipated his fear. What a great example of how faith triumphs over fear! Thomas's faith freed him from any fear, He took no thought for himself, even to the point of dying. How often do we overlook Thomas's brave faith and go straight to his weakness? I, too, need the faith of Thomas found in John 11. So how do we get it?

Second Timothy 1:7 tells us God does not give us a spirit of fear but a spirit of power and love and self-discipline. How might these traits look in our lives?

The second thing striking me is Thomas's role as an influencer. He encouraged the disciples to go along with him and die for Jesus. Recently, as I prepared to redecorate the house, I discovered an online influencer, or there is no telling how all of it would have turned out. When anyone compliments the new décor, in my heart I know I am in no way responsible, but some "best friend I never met" convinced me what I should do. That's just what an influencer does. It was Thomas, the Influencer, who convinced the disciples to go with Jesus. How seldom do we consider Thomas this way?

What does 1 Thessalonians 5:11 tell us about encouraging others?

So, in chapter 11 we find "Brave Thomas" and "Encouraging Thomas," but does anyone ever refer to him by these nicknames? Most likely not. Should anyone say to you, "Don't be like Thomas," take a moment to savor this man's redeeming qualities and be sure to respond with, "Thank you!"

Now, take a deep breath as we prepare for the train wreck of Thomas's weakest moment.

Thomas's Face of Doubt

For three years, Thomas had walked and talked and eaten and communed with Jesus. He had witnessed mind-blowing, faith-building miracles and soaked up the Savior's bold sermons. Sadly, Thomas did not go down in history for his unwavering faith. Instead, this apostle's legacy was derived from one single chapter that labeled him with his unfortunate nickname, "Doubting Thomas." So, let's dive into the real meat of this story and read John 20. Again, record your thoughts on the notes page.

Yes, chapter 20 justifies why this apostle was dubbed, "Doubting Thomas." This account, however, leaves unanswered questions. Once at a mother-daughter dinner, when asked to describe the mothers in one word, my daughter replied, "curious." I totally own that! Because of my curiosity, my own notes page contains lots of questions. The first was, "Why was Thomas not with the disciples following Jesus' crucifixion?" Was Thomas so distraught, he needed time to process and heal? Was Thomas filled with so much fear, he hid? There simply are no answers, but if strength is found in numbers, sadly Thomas was separated from his strong village.

Here is another of my questions on my notes page. "Why did the risen Savior choose to preserve His wounds when He returned from the dead?" Surely, if He could be raised to new life, He could have also been raised free from the wounds of crucifixion. But, perhaps Jesus considered how we, humans, crave affirmation. Those wounds stood as proof of His deity. His scars indicated without a shadow of a doubt that the same Jesus who went into the tomb dead was the same Jesus who came out of the tomb alive. The Lord understood our peace that comes from proof.

Why did the risen Savior choose to preserve His wounds when He returned from the dead?

Oh, to have been a fly on the wall when Thomas rejoined the disciples and learned they had been with the risen Jesus. Surely Thomas sat wide-eyed as the disciples all talked at once, telling of their incredible visit with the Savior. Did he gasp aloud as they spoke of seeing the holes in His hands from nails of the cross and the gash in His side from the Roman's sword.

Now, here comes the "doubting" part. As Thomas opened his mouth and responded to the claim of a risen Jesus, he began with one poignant word. . .

Unless

It was the first word out of Thomas's mouth, and it was a game-changer! *Unless* spoke to the weakest part of Thomas' faith in the power of Jesus to overcome death. With that one word, *Unless*, Thomas laid down a demand of Jesus. Thomas was not about to believe the unbelievable *unless* he, too, could see and touch Jesus' wounds as proof. When Thomas doubted Jesus to be alive, he was doubting in the deity of Jesus and the power of God. And so it was, with that one word, *Unless*, Thomas's unfortunate legacy was sealed.

A Spider Web or a Strong Wall?

There is a story of a WWII soldier, who during a time of intense fighting, was separated from his unit. To avoid enemy capture, he climbed a ridge and hid in one of its numerous small caves. Being a Christian, he prayed for deliverance. *Lord, please protect me from the enemy. But if You do not, know I still love You and trust You.* He lay quietly as the enemy began to climb the ridge, in search of him. He soon noticed a spider had begun to weave a web over the entrance of his cave. *How ironic,* he thought. *I need God to build me a strong wall of protection and instead I get a spider's web.*

From his hidden vantage point, the soldier watched the enemy advance, inspecting each cave. When it seemed his capture was inevitable, he prepared for one final stand. However, as the enemy turned toward his cave, the sun reflected off that spider web, giving the appearance no one had entered his cave in quite some time. With that assumption, the enemy soldiers turned away and continued their search in a different direction.

Father, forgive me for doubting You, he prayed, *for with You, a spider web is as strong as a wall of protection.* That soldier lived to tell of the power and protection Jesus provided.

When we consider God's power at work in our lives, do we see a spider web or a strong wall of protection? Do we doubt the truth of Luke 1:37, *"For with God nothing will be impossible."* Or do we trust God's power to have no limits, being assured both His spider webs and His strong walls are equally able to protect us.

The old saying, "Seeing is believing," rings true for humans. But according to Scripture, faith is not found in the affirmation of seeing. What does Hebrews 11:1 tell us about faith?

True faith is believing in things we cannot see, and Thomas was filled with true faith in chapter 11. But where was that now? Let's recall the events leading up to chapter 20, because they might shed some light on Thomas's doubts.

When faith moves out, fear and doubt find plenty of room to move in.

Jesus had been arrested, tortured, nailed to a cross, and taken His final breath. This cruelest of deaths was openly witnessed and came as a shock to the disciples who never clearly understood the entirety of Christ's mission. So, the three days between the cross and the resurrection were the most hopeless of days. Was Thomas so discouraged by the events of the cross that he failed to see any possibility for resurrection? Perhaps a sense of hopelessness meant Thomas needed solitude. Maybe the apostles kept discussing it all and Thomas was too distraught to listen anymore. Whatever his reason for separating from the apostles, Thomas's faith was shaken by the events he witnessed. And when faith moves out, fear and doubt find plenty of room to move in.

Ephesians 6:10-18 tells us all about our Christian armor and refers to our "shield of faith." Did you know a shield serves as the first barrier of defense against attack and will defend us against any arrows of doubt? Perhaps Thomas had laid his shield of faith down and, in doing so, found himself pierced by the flaming arrows of doubt from the evil one.

Before we are too harsh on Thomas, we might consider that he simply desired the same tangible proof the other apostles had already received. Thomas wanted to see and touch the wounds, too. The rest had. I have often wondered, if the other apostles had not seen nor touched the Savior's crucifixion wounds, would they, too, have doubted? Would "Skeptical Simon," and "Apprehensive Andrew" have gone down in history with "Doubting Thomas"?

When we doubt our Savior, perhaps we, too, have laid down our shield of faith and allowed our weakest link to be captured. Thomas was a man committed to the Savior, yet he struggled with his faith journey. Because of his moment of doubt, we tend to overlook his positives and label him by his weakest moment. We humans are so quick to see the worst in others.

But remember, it was not Jesus who assigned Thomas that title, "Doubting Thomas." We did that!

Others Who Doubted

Thomas was not alone in doubting God. Recall our study of Eve? She allowed the evil one to place a seed of doubt in her heart. Seeds of doubt quickly root and produce offspring. Seeds of doubt grow into fields of doubt and change the landscape of our beautiful faith gardens.

Consider others who fell prey to doubt:

- Saul doubted his ability to be king and **hid** among the baggage (1 Samuel 10).

- Jonah doubted God had the best plan and he **ran away**. (Jonah 1).

- Moses doubted his ability to lead a nation and became the master at **making excuses** (Exodus 3-4).

- Sarah doubted God's power to give her a child and **laughed** at its absurdity (Genesis 18).

- Gideon doubted his ability to be a mighty warrior and **required affirmation** (Judges 6).

- Zechariah doubted God would give him a son an **lost his voice** (Luke 1).

Doubts Tangle Up Our Lives

For a moment, let us look inward. In times of doubt, do we, like Saul, hide from God's purpose for us? Like Jonah, do we run from what we feel demands too much of us? Like Moses, do excuses flow like waterfalls from our lips when asked to do the hard jobs? Like Sarah, do we think it humorous when God claims He will do the impossible in our lives? Like Gideon, do we fail to trust God's providence unless we see God's evidence? And like Zechariah, do doubts stop our tongues from spreading God's message? Yes, doubt invades our lives with purpose and plan.

When we doubt God's forgiveness of our sins, or His desire to redeem us, or His grace that flows so freely, we make light of the sacrifice of Jesus. We question the validity of the cross. We say without realizing it, the blood He shed was not good enough, and His suffering was unnecessary.

A Final Thought on Thomas

Settle in real comfy now for one last story as we wrap up "Doubting Thomas," and as we put the finishing touches on all our heroes of faith whose lives have guided us.

Every morning, I rise to make the bed, toss in a load of laundry, and dash out the door. Sadly, I often overlook the many blessings of my loving God. Gratefully, the short 28 words recorded in 2 Corinthians 9:8 help remind me.

*"And God is able to bless you abundantly, so that in **ALL** things at **ALL** times, having **ALL** that you need, you will abound in **EVERY** good work"* (NIV).

Notice the repetitive use of the word, *all*. What a daring word because it allows no room for exceptions. For this reason, *all* should be used sparingly. However, the Holy Spirit used it freely; *all* things, *all* times, *all* that you need, and *every* good work (a synonym of *all*). These are God-breathed words from a God who cannot lie, and He assures us there are no limits to the ways He will bless us.

I recall an ice cream party my husband and I hosted. I took this event seriously, choosing each flavor and topping carefully. The result was the most amazing ice cream buffet ever witnessed, if I do say so myself. (Totally Pinterest-worthy!) There were varieties of flavors, toppings, whipped creams, glazes, fruits, nuts, and of course, cherries to adorn the top. I received so much pleasure choosing each treat, and I was confident my guests would delight in all the options.

The ice cream party was a hit—that is, for all but one. One guest surveyed the ice cream buffet before he picked up a bowl, dipped out a single scoop of vanilla, and turned to depart. I almost accosted him mid-step because I could not fathom his passing over the remaining 64 items. I asked him which toppings he might like on that plain vanilla, and he replied, "None, thank you. I just want a scoop of vanilla."

I choked back the urge to say, "Did you overlook the macadamia nut ice cream, or the homemade almond-flavored whipped cream, or the made-from-scratch warm blueberry drizzle? And what about a cherry on top? However, by the grace of God I simply replied, "Enjoy!" and choked down the remainder of what I was tempted to say.

In the same way, are we guilty of bypassing the goodness God—the goodness He lovingly provides and delights in giving us? His love, mercy, forgiveness, grace, joy, and peace are all free at His table and free for our taking. God's table is filled to overflowing with every good gift imaginable, and doubt will not be served there.

How do we use God's gifts? Well, for us to profess our Savior to the unbeliever, God provides us helpings of boldness and truth. To raise godly children, God allows us an extra scoop of wisdom, strength, and patience. To move beyond our past sins, we find a sweet helping of peace that only His forgiveness provides. To enjoy a close and loving relationship with God, trust is waiting at His table. These delights and many more are waiting for us to scoop them up. So, friend, lay aside all doubts and pick up the biggest bowl you can find. Circle God's table and fill up. Prepare to be amazed at the ways your life will glorify God through His blessings.

And as we close, remember dear friend, Jesus did not label His dear apostle as "Doubting Thomas." That unfortunate nickname was carved into stone by those of us who defined Thomas by his weakest moment.

Prepare to be amazed at the ways your life will glorify God through His blessings.

Notes

Father God, forgive us when we overlook Your blessings. Help us to fill up on Your goodness. Give us the strength to relinquish our doubts and insecurities to You. And thank You for refusing to label us by our weakest moments.

Notes

Notes

Notes